MW00364765

TEXAS HAUNTED FORTS

TEXAS HAUNTED FORTS

SECOND EDITION

ELAINE COLEMAN

Globe
Pequot

Guilford, Connecticut

I am proud to dedicate this book to my mother and father, Bessie and Calvin Laird, who instilled in me the mettle to get the job done and do it right. I love you more than you'll ever know.

Globe Pequot

An imprint of The Rowman & Littlefield Publishing Group, Inc.
4501 Forbes Blvd., Ste. 200
Lanham, MD 20706
www.rowman.com

Distributed by NATIONAL BOOK NETWORK

Copyright © 2018 by Elaine Coleman
All photos by the author unless otherwise noted.

All rights reserved. No part of this book may be reproduced in any form or by any electronic or mechanical means, including information storage and retrieval systems, without written permission from the publisher, except by a reviewer who may quote passages in a review.

British Library Cataloguing in Publication Information available
Library of Congress Cataloging-in-Publication Data available

ISBN 978-1-4930-3245-7 (paperback)
ISBN 978-1-4930-3246-4 (e-book)

♾™ The paper used in this publication meets the minimum requirements of American National Standard for Information Sciences—Permanence of Paper for Printed Library Materials, ANSI/NISO Z39.48-1992.

Printed in the United States of America

CONTENTS

OK

AR

NM

Fort Elliott ■
○ **Amarillo**

Fort Buffalo Springs ■
Fort
Fitzhugh ■   ■ Fort Lyday
Fort Richardson ■
Camp Cooper ■   ■ Fort Belknap   ■ Fort
Sherman
Fort Phantom Hill ■   Fort Griffin ■   Fort Bird ■
                Fort ■ **Fort Worth** ○
                        Dallas ○

Camp Elizabeth ■   Fort ■ Blair's Fort ■
                Chadbourne
Fort Bliss ■   Camp ■ Fort Graham ■   ■ Fort Parker
El Paso   Camp Charlotte ■   Colorado   **Waco** ○
Fort Hancock ■   ■ Fort Concho   Fort Gates ■
Fort Quitman ■   Real Presidio ■   ■ Fort Milam/Fort Burleson
            de San Sabá   Little River ■ Fort Boggy
Fort Stockton ■   Fort McKavett ■   Fort ■ Fort
        Fort   Fort   Mason   Croghan
Fort Davis ■   Lancaster   Fort Terrett ■
Fort D. A. Russell ■   Fort Martin ■ ⊕**Austin**
Fort Cienega ■   Scott   Fort Colorado ■   ■ Moore's Fort
                Woods' Fort ■   **Houston** ○   Fort Anahuac ■
Fort Leaton ■   ■ Camp Hudson   **San**   Fort Bend ■
            Antonio
        Fort Clark ■   ○ ■ The Alamo
            Fort
        Fort   Lincoln   Fort St. Louis ■
        Inge
    Fort ■
    Duncan   Fort Esperanza ■
Mexico   Fort Lipantitlán ■   Fort Marcy ■
        Fort McIntosh ■

Gulf of
Mexico

Fort Ringgold ■

Fort Brown ■

LA

N

| 0 | 150 | 300 kilometers |
| 0 | 150 | 300 miles |

TEXAS FORTS

CONTENTS

ACKNOWLEDGMENTS

The help I received from the many individuals while writing this book came from too many sources to mention by name. Some wish to remain anonymous. Therefore, I am going to thank everyone who helped make this book possible.

A special appreciation goes to the librarians, staff members at the state parks I visited, and, most importantly, those folks who were willing to share stories of ghosts known to them personally.

Special thanks to Grace Bennett, Robert L. Boerne, Juanita Hill, Conrad McClure, Robin Street, Buddy Garza, and Kurt Kemp for your firsthand information. I truly believe you are the heart and the soul of the legends of your respective forts.

I want to thank Dixie and Desmond Powell for showing Jerry and me around at Fort Concho and loaning me that marvelous book.

Another group without whom I could not have completed this book: JoAnne Horn, Robyn Conley-O'Brien, Sue Turner, Gwen Choate, and Maurice Mallow—thank you. You ladies were my inspiration and my cheering section. If not for you, there would not be a book. Thanks for being there when I needed your special encouragement.

I want to thank my husband, Jerry, for putting up with my crazy timetable and not complaining about the phantom meals I never prepared. Thanks, I love you. To my children, Racheal, Rebecca, their husbands, and the grandchildren, thank you for encouraging me.

INTRODUCTION

My fascination with ghosts began when I was a child. My grandfather would tell me if I didn't behave, he would have the ghost
of Rube's old bull come and get me. I always wanted to see that
ghost bull.

My family moved to the country in 1972. My father worked
at night, and my mother, brother, and sister and I would sit around
the fireplace at night with the lights off, telling ghost stories until
bedtime. Some nights we drove down the lane from the house,
where trees overlapped above us, and told our ghost stories.

On our property I found a cave, and I explored that hole in the
wall of the mountain several times. I found relics such as pottery
shards and an old spoon. Carved into the wall was Belle Starr's
name. I imagined the lady outlaw's ghost lived in the cave and she
would someday speak to me.

Once on Halloween night, my friends and I visited an old
Indian cemetery. We witnessed a blue light floating behind us, and
we left in a hurry. I wanted to return to see what it was that didn't
want us there, but my friends were afraid.

Legends of Texas that make up our heritage are sometimes
fact and sometimes fiction. For as long as I can remember, I have
craved the knowledge to speak to the ghosts and legends of the
past. Through my study of history, I feel I have, to an extent. These
cravings for information have helped me on my quest to separate
fact from fiction. It is my hope that the stories within these pages
are an equal mixture of both.

PART I

FORTS ESTABLISHED
BEFORE 1800

FORT ST. LOUIS/PRESIDIO DE LA BAHÍA (FORT DEFIANCE)

Fort St. Louis has a long history dating from 1685, when the first explorers from France came to the wilderness that would someday be known as Texas and built the first known settlement on the west side of Garcitas Creek.

In 1687, at the original site of Fort St. Louis, the French explorer La Salle glanced back as he and his men marched into the untamed Texas wilderness. He tried to still the nagging fear in his mind that all would not be well with the settlement he left behind. The Karankawa Indians had attacked the settlement some twenty times in the previous two years, and he felt they would do so again, as soon as he and his army were out of sight.

Two years after La Salle left the settlement, the Karankawas once more attacked and destroyed Fort St. Louis. All but five of the twenty men, women, and children were killed.

The Indian women tried to save the wife and three-month-old child of Lt. Gabriel Barbier, the fort's commander, but the warriors bound the woman and made her watch while they tortured and killed her baby. The violence did not end with the murder of the child. Barbier's wife was tortured and killed by the same warriors.

The children who survived the vicious massacre at Fort St. Louis in 1689 were enslaved in the Karankawa Indian village. After being rescued by the Alonso De Leon expedition, nine-year-old John Baptiste Talon, one of the children enslaved by the Indians, gave the only eyewitness account of the massacre at Fort St. Louis. He told of the brutality that Barbier's wife and child suffered.

It is said that her ghost still roams the area surrounding the original site of Fort St. Louis. During quiet nights, she can be heard weeping, mournfully calling out her husband's name, begging him to save her and their child.

Presidio Nuestro Señora de Loreto de la Bahía was established at the site of the abandoned Fort St. Louis in April 1721. Later, the fort was relocated and reestablished several times between 1726 and 1749, until its final move to its present location.

When Texans under the command of Col. James Walker Fannin took over the fort in 1836, they renamed it Fort Defiance. The men suffered a devastating defeat at the hands of General Santa Anna's troops. Santa Anna promptly ordered the execution of Fannin and his troops. The executions of the 342 men were carried out a short distance from the fort's walls, and the men's bodies were stacked and burned. Eventually the proud Texans were buried in a mass grave. The fort now stands as a monument to the Texas soldiers who were killed in the bloodiest massacre of the Texas Revolution.

Recently, while visiting the Presidio de la Bahía during a Cinco de Mayo celebration, my friend Sam and I were stunned to see the handsome blond figure of Fannin walking among the participants of the parade. When we approached him, he smiled sadly at us and disappeared into the crowd.

During that same visit, the chapel bells rang loud and clear through the morning air while several other visitors at the fort compound hurried to reach the small building. All was quiet and serene as we sat solemnly, deep in prayer.

This memorial was erected on the site of a mass grave where Texas heroes lie at Presidio de la Bahía/Goliad.

As I sat in the small church I noticed a tall woman dressed in black entering the chapel. A blast of cold air swept over my shoulders. Slowly, the woman glided to the altar of the chapel and lit a candle for lost souls. Kneeling, she began to cry. As her sobs of grief increased in volume, I got to my feet and tiptoed to her, hoping to give her comfort. The air surrounding the woman was extremely cold. Paying little attention to that, I gently reached out to the woman and asked if there was anything I could do for her. When my hand touched her shoulder, the mysterious woman in black disappeared into a cloud of mist. Stunned by what happened, I stood motionless for a moment, and then I went in search of more information about this woman and who she was.

I learned that every few years this same scene is replayed in the chapel and other areas of the fort grounds. Apparently, no one knows who the woman in black might be or for whom she grieves, but one thing is certain: The candles she lights continue to burn long after she disappears.

The chapel at Presidio de la Bahía THE LYDA HILL TEXAS COLLECTION OF
PHOTOGRAPHS IN CAROL M. HIGHSMITH'S AMERICA PROJECT, LIBRARY OF CONGRESS,
PRINTS AND PHOTOGRAPHS DIVISION

According to some people I talked with, she is seen on the
grounds early in the mornings when only the caretaker is out making his rounds, but she is not the only early morning visitor to the
fort. An ex-caretaker has also witnessed two men dueling on the
grounds of the Presidio de la Bahía. He reports that every so often
around the time of the new moon, dawn's light filters through the
leaves of the oak trees. He can see the lady in black standing at the
edge of the trees just in the shadows, watching across the dew-
covered grass, her eyes piercing the filtered light.

The caretaker said he stood mesmerized while he watched two
other shadowy figures dance to the ringing of swords. Parry and
thrust. Parry and thrust. Each Spanish soldier took the slightest

advantage left by the other. Sweat dripped from the soldiers' faces in the cool morning air. Neither gave any evidence of knowledge that they were being watched, intent on only one outcome: death.

A movement in the trees and the crack of a fallen limb distracted one of the soldiers, leaving him vulnerable to his opponent's sword. He fell to the ground, and the sound of loud weeping echoed through the fog. The lady in black vanished into the background, and the soldiers faded into nothingness.

Upon searching the clearing, the caretaker found no sign of the recent bloody battle. There was no trampled grass and there were no bloodstains on the earth. Nothing was visible to suggest that what he saw was real or merely a trick of his imagination. Many people I talked to have told of seeing the ghost of a headless Texas soldier riding through the compound atop a majestic white stallion, as well.

The tall, misty figure wears high leather boots, cream-colored pants, and a full-sleeved white linen shirt. A long red scarf, where his head had once been, flaps in the wind. As the rider's ghostly horse reaches the wall, the lady in black appears holding her hands to her face, and her weeping grows louder, filling the air. Mysteriously, the rider and the white stallion gallop through her and blend into the shadows, not to be seen again until the night of the next full moon.

Several other people tell of the soldiers buried near the mission's old stone church. Many of them believe that one or more of these soldiers compel another ghostly woman to search the camp compound. She's been seen dressed in a flowing white shroud. She floats across the compound late on cold misty nights, searching for her husband and child buried nearby.

The groundskeeper told me of becoming acquainted with a visitor to the park who told him that he'd heard men's frantic voices and sorrowful moans of pain and suffering coming from the area of the 1836 massacre. He reported the smell of human decay as well as voices and the sound of footsteps on the wooden planks

The cannon at Presidio de la Bahía stands as a reminder of the men who fought and perished for freedom.

of a nearby bridge. Step for step, he was followed. He turned to see who was walking behind him, but no one was there. However, when he continued walking, the footsteps started again. The man had camped on the park grounds the night before but refused to stay another night.

Others reported witnessing a young woman with black hair flowing down her back. She carries a baby wrapped in a blanket. They call her La Llorna, the Weeping Woman. She roams the darkness crying over her dead baby.

Presidio de la Bahía is located two miles south of Goliad, Texas, on US Highway 183 (77A). Presidio de la Bahía was established at this location in 1749, with Mission Espíritu Santo. It has been owned by the Catholic Church since 1853 and is currently operated by the Catholic Diocese of Victoria, Texas.

Mrs. Thomas O'Connor, owner and custodian, began restoration of the Presidio de la Bahía on April 24, 1963. She did this for the Corpus Christi Diocese of the Catholic Church. The work was done under the direction of architect Raiford L. Stripling and a staff of restoration technicians headed by engineer L. A. Pettus, archaeologist R. E. Beard, and superintendent O. G. Compton. They all had experience in the investigation, restoration, and preservation of the nearby contemporary historic sites of Mission Espíritu Santo and Mission Rosario. Reverend Edward Kircher was a representative of Bishop M. S. Garriga and Monsignor Wm. J. Oberste on the work. He also supervised the labor and was the fiscal agent for the Kathryn O'Connor Foundation.

Presidio de la Bahía is located in the heart of South Texas, two miles south of Goliad off US Highway 183/77A.

THE ALAMO

The Alamo has long been the symbol of Texas pride. The ghosts of many of the heroes who died at the old mission still roam the plaza. From as far back as at least 1836, apparitions have been seen at the Alamo.

Father Antonio Olivares established the Mission San Antonio de Valero in 1718. The mission served the settlers and Indians alike until 1803, when the Spanish cavalry took over the mission and named it Alamo de Parras. At the battle of San Jacinto in 1836, Santa Anna knew capture was imminent. He called one of his most trusted servants to his side. Instructing the man to fade into the surroundings, Santa Anna dispatched a message to General Andrade.

General Andrade had been sent to replace Santa Anna, to clean up after the battle of the Alamo, and to make sure no other uprisings from the Texans would occur. Santa Anna's servant arrived with his master's orders in hand just as Andrade was about to leave the area.

In the message, Santa Anna told Andrade to destroy the Mission San Antonio de Valero, the Alamo. Destroy and leave not a stone standing. Organizing his troops for their march to the Rio Grande, Andrade commanded Colonel Sanchez and his men to carry out Santa Anna's demands.

According to reports, as Sanchez and his troops approached the old chapel, all that remained of the mission, they were confronted with six diablos or ghostly monks. These apparitions emerged from the walls of the mission waving flaming swords over their heads, advancing toward the soldiers, and shouting, "Do not touch the walls of the Alamo!"

Quickly, Colonel Sanchez, eyes bugged and sweat dripping from his face, crossed his chest and stumbled backwards into his second in command.

"Help me on my horse, we must leave here immediately." The frightened colonel and his men spurred their animals and rushed back to the camp, reporting the events to General Andrade in stuttering broken sentences. Upset with the cowardly Colonel Sanchez, General Andrade took several men and one cannon with him to the old mission. He cantered his horse up to the chapel and shouted orders for his troops to aim the cannon at the front of the chapel. He was about to give the order to fire when the ghostly monks appeared with their fiery swords. The apparitions shouted their warnings. Their moaning voices were enough to startle the general's horse, causing it to rear and unseat him.

General Andrade caught the reins of his horse and turned to his men, who were already in retreat. Looking back at the chapel, then to the long barracks, he watched wide-eyed as smoke and flames erupted from the barracks and the ground. The smoke took form into a large image of a man standing heads above him. The massive form held balls of fire in both hands and, like an avenging angel, cast them at the general. Andrade fled the mission with his men. No one has ever harmed the mission again.

Folks believe that the ghosts of the soldiers killed at the Alamo manifested into the large spirit to protect their resting place.

When I visited the Alamo as a teenager with a friend of mine, being typical teenagers, we looked for the strange and unusual everywhere we went. Sherry's parents bought us tour tickets, and we toured the various missions in the area, including the Alamo.

The Alamo THE LYDA HILL TEXAS COLLECTION OF PHOTOGRAPHS IN CAROL M. HIGHSMITH'S AMERICA PROJECT, LIBRARY OF CONGRESS, PRINTS AND PHOTOGRAPHS DIVISION

Walking along behind the crowd from the bus, we got left outside. Sherry glanced up toward the top of the chapel and drew in a quick breath. Pointing toward the upper windows, she grabbed my arm and hoarsely whispered, "Look up there and tell me what you see. Is it a fire? It looks like smoke."

I figured she was pulling one of her dramatic tricks on me, and I slowly gazed upward and asked, "What is it, the building on fire or something?" Shaking my head, unable to tear my gaze away from the image in the window, I whispered back to her, "There's no smoke or fire, Sherry. There's a little boy standing on that window frame. He says he's looking for his family."

"What? Are you nuts?"

"No, look. See, he's reaching out to us. He needs help. He's looking for his parents."

Sherry, seemingly disgusted with me, pulled me toward the doorway, where we went inside.

"Wait!" I cried out. "Didn't you see that little blond-haired boy in the window? You saw something, didn't you?" It worried me that I had seen the boy but Sherry hadn't.

"I thought I saw smoke coming out of that top window, that's all. I sure didn't see any little boy up there."

Sherry pulled on my arm, and we rejoined the tour group. The whole time I was inside the Alamo, I felt I was being watched and I could hear voices, low whispers, from the walls and darkened corners of the old mission. I was jumpy, and Sherry was getting on my nerves.

As we completed the tour and started back toward the bus, I turned for one more look, and there, high above the plaza, the little boy floated on the edge of the window ledge.

Years later, when I returned to the Alamo on a late February afternoon, I again saw the little blond-haired boy, and I knew then I had not been a crazy teenager. Upon my most recent visit to the Alamo, I talked with several employees who confirmed the image of the child in the window as well as other incidents taking place in and around the plaza.

For instance, midday in late spring, one of the Alamo rangers made his rounds, checking to make sure all was well in the plaza. It was one of those really hot spring days in South Texas, and he had taken his hat off to wipe the sweat from his brow. Putting his hat back on, he saw a suspicious-looking man walking across the grounds toward the library.

The ranger took note of the man's strange attire: He wore black boots, a black plantation-style hat, and a long black over-coat. Keeping his distance, he followed the man until he reached the shadows of the chapel building, where he saw the figure fade away.

The ranger hurried after the stranger, but he found no one hiding in the shadows and discovered no footprints in the flower beds. Checking with other employees at the Alamo, he came up empty-handed as no one else had seen the peculiar man. The ranger realized the apparel was not something of present-day wear. He described what he'd seen to another ranger, who thought the attire was from the 1830s.

Since that time others have seen the same apparition strolling through the plaza in broad daylight as well as at night. One school teacher told of her unusual experience at the Alamo on a rainy day in February.

The bellies of the darkening clouds appeared as if they would burst at any time. Jagged lightning flashed closer to the plaza with each strike, and thunder rolled across the threatening skies of South Texas. A downpour was imminent. A few courageous citizens roamed the sidewalks in front of the Alamo, touring the town with friends or family. A school bus rolled to a stop in front of the old mission, and a group of children with several teachers stepped off as the rain began to pepper the plaza. The teachers hurried the children inside the main Alamo building so they wouldn't get wet.

As the last teacher stepped inside, she looked back and saw two ladies in ankle-length dresses like women wore in the 1700s. One's fabric-covered bonnet, trimmed with ribbons and flowers, hid her face. The other woman was attired in a full-length cloak, covering her dress completely, gathered onto a lace-edged hood. The ladies didn't seem to be in a hurry; they simply walked at a steady pace, their heads down and faces hidden from the rain.

Lightning flashed, striking the ground and then burning across the sky. The smaller woman dropped to the ground. Her companion fell to her knees and began screaming for help, but the thunderous racket in the sky kept anyone else from hearing the cries. Bending over her friend on the ground, the woman wept. The teacher, who witnessed the bizarre scene, started out into the rain to help as a streak of lightning split the skies followed by a clash of thunder. At that moment, the women disappeared. The teacher found a gold ring lying on the plaza stones that was charred ever so slightly.

On my most recent visit to the Alamo, I noticed a shadowy figure near an old tree in the middle of the plaza just outside the gift shop. I asked my daughter and granddaughters if they saw the figure, but none of them saw what I did. They think I am warped because I seem to see these things and no one else can, but this was real.

More tales of ghostly sightings can be heard when talking to the staff and people who have visited the old mission.

Everyone remembers The Alamo. It is the story that is bigger than even Texas itself. The Daughters of the Republic of Texas have worked tirelessly to keep the historic monument of Texas's independence intact. The Alamo is located in the heart of San Antonio, along the River Walk, one of San Antonio's most beautiful attractions. Drive to San Antonio, Texas, and then follow the overhead signs to find the Alamo.

REAL PRESIDIO DE SAN SABÁ

Soldiers were sent to protect the original Real Presidio de San Sabá, built of stone in April 1757, and the nearby mission stockade, erected on the east bank of the San Sabá River, sporting buildings constructed of wood and logs. The mission, also known as San Luis de las Amarillas, served nearly four hundred settlers as well as a few Apache Indians working as servants to the priests and settlers.

In March 1758, a Comanche raiding party swooped down on the settlement and took a large herd of horses. This is when Colonel Parrilla called his troops to general quarters and sent orders to evacuate the mission. The priests were to gather the residents to the Real Presidio de San Sabá until such time as it was safe to go back to the mission, after the full moon, known by the native Indians as the Comanche Moon.

Father Alonso Giraldo de Terreros, president of the mission, refused to leave the mission unprotected. His goal was to civilize all the savage Indians on the prairie, including the Apache and the Comanche. After a heated argument between Colonel Parrilla and the father-president, Terreros agreed to evacuate the mission on the following day.

The morning dawned bright and clear, but the missionaries and settlers were awakened to the bloodcurdling war cries of some two thousand Comanche Indians. The Comanches gave no quarter, killing and wounding as many settlers as possible. They killed two of the three priests who guided the settlers.

Fray Miguel de Molina lay quietly hidden under fodder straw near the stock pens where the horses and donkeys milled about. Clutching his rosary, he prayed to the Blessed Virgin Mary, hoping he would not be heard over the screams of agony and the bloodthirsty war cries of the savage Comanche Indians.

He prayed that the soldiers in the presidio across the river could hear the screams and would come to the rescue of those in the mission. He knew if the soldiers at the presidio heard, they would want to help, but they were so few he didn't look for them to rescue the settlers.

The battle calmed and Fray Molina peeked out through the straw of his hiding place and watched in horror as the Comanches surrounded the kneeling priest, Fray Jose de Santiesteban. Molina could hardly suppress his screams of terror when the Indians beheaded his friend. Burrowing deeper into the straw, Fray Molina held his rosary close to his lips and whispered another prayer for the soul of Fray Santiesteban. Frightened to the depth of his soul, he glanced through the straw again and saw the resident Apaches and one soldier slipping away from the destroyed mission and the savage Comanches. Surely they would send help from the presidio. Time passed slowly and the sound of Fray Santiesteban's gurgling death replayed in Molina's mind.

As quickly as the Comanches came, they left the mission, leaving in their wake destruction and death. All was quiet once more, and Fray Molina peered out from his cover to make certain the savages no longer occupied the mission walls. Heartbroken by the carnage and destruction of his beloved mission, he set out to find survivors.

After searching a short time, he found a few residents of the mission huddled together under a pile of charred debris. Urging the terrified people to leave their hiding place, he whispered, "Come along, my children. We must leave at once for the Real Presidio de San Sabá, lest the savage Comanches return."

One woman's leg had been broken when the wall of a hut had fallen on her. Fray Molina carried her. The others, most of them wounded, followed quietly, still in shock from the carnage and the horrible deaths they had witnessed.

Stealing away from the destroyed mission under the cover of darkness, the priest and his ragtag group stayed close to the underbrush before attempting to cross the river. Molina whispered to the residents he had come to love as his family and showed them what to do in order to get across the river without being detected by the Comanches. He cut limbs from a nearby bush and stuck them behind a parishioner's head and then down into the back of his blouse.

"Now, that is better. You look just like a bush from the back now. The Comanches will have a hard time distinguishing you from the foliage along the riverbanks.

"Fording the San Sabá will be the easiest part of our midnight journey to safety. The Comanches could be waiting on the other side of the river to attack us again and if so we must run and hide wherever we can."

Fray Molina spoke quietly. "The only chance we have is to reach the Real Presidio de San Sabá and the protection of Colonel Parrilla and his soldiers. Say a silent prayer and let's get going." Fray Molina directed his small band of survivors across the San Sabá River. Once on dry ground, he led them to the cover of the brush lining the west bank, talking in low soothing tones the whole time.

"Remember now, there is the possibility that the Comanches are still about, so we must make a run for the presidio," Molina

The solid rock walls of Real Presidio de San Sabá offered protection to survivors of the horrific massacre at the San Luis de las Amarillas mission.

announced. He knelt beside the woman with the broken leg and gave her a strip of cloth.

"If the pain becomes too severe, put this in your mouth and bite down on it. You must not cry out, whatever you do."

Nodding, the woman did as she was told and placed the cloth between her teeth.

The distance from the river to the presidio was not so great, but it was all open ground. The full moon shone down on the shortened grasses of early spring, doing little to offer him and his flock any protection. Molina could see the silhouettes of the soldiers on top of the presidio standing with rifles ready. Once they got close enough to the walls of the fort, Fray Molina cried out for the soldiers not to fire their weapons.

After reaching the safety of the high walls of the presidio, Fray Molina reported the atrocities he had witnessed to Colonel Parrilla. Later, he asked for a room where he could seek solace and pray for the souls of the lost parishioners and the two priests who had died in the massacre.

He never overcame the heartbreak of the savagery dealt to his fellow priests and the others in the mission. The horrible image of his friends, one being beheaded and the other slashed into dozens of pieces, was more than his tortured mind could bear.

Day and night, his whispered words of prayer and the rosary beads, clicking together, could be heard throughout the encampment. Day after day, he refused food, citing self-inflicted punishment as the reason for his refusal to eat.

After a three-day wait to make sure the Comanches weren't returning to the mission, the time came to bury the dead. Colonel Parrilla begged Fray Molina to stay at the presidio. Weakened from the ordeal of the massacre, coupled with exhaustion and lack of food, and barely able to walk, Fray Molina insisted on going back to the mission.

"Since I did not prevent the massacre, I can at least attend to the dead."

"You are a stubborn man, Fray Molina," Colonel Parrilla said. "What happened at the mission was not your fault. Father Terreros refused to abandon the mission when I reported impending disaster. The blame must lie with the father-president of the mission."

"But I hid myself away, like a coward. I watched the Comanches ride into the mission and massacre my friends and fellow man. Instead of trying to help the poor souls who died, I hid away in terror and cried like a baby."

In his mind, Fray Molina still envisioned Fray Jose's head rolling across the blood-soaked ground. He remembered the bloodlust in the eyes of savages who had killed so easily. Those images stood out in the nightmares he lived through night after night.

Because of the attack on the mission, all Spanish settlements were thrown into a panic. No one, especially the underpaid soldiers, was willing to leave the safety of the Real Presidio de San Sabá garrison to help protect the surrounding settlements. Some soldiers stated that if the settlers were foolish enough to come to this barren land, then they should defend themselves.

Captain Rabago, the new commander of the presidio, took command in 1766 and requested permission to destroy a French fortress on the Red River several hundred miles away. The Comanches sought help from the French there, but Captain Rabago's superiors thought they knew best, and the request was denied.

By 1767, the Spanish government ordered that all horses were to be removed from Real Presidio de San Sabá and later, due to another Comanche raid in June 1768, it was abandoned. The relinquishment of the Real Presidio de San Sabá heralded the end of Spain's political and military strength in Texas.

The land between the Rio Grande and San Antonio was pretty much left to the roving bands of hostile Comanches, Lipan Apaches, Kiowas, Karankawas, and the other nomadic tribes of Texas upon the abandonment of the fort.

Real Presidio de San Sabá holds many secrets and spirits. Upon visiting the presidio on the evening of the Comanche Moon, the ghostly sound of clicking beads and whispers could be heard from across the river. Darkness rolled in from the brush, and my friend and I listened to quiet prayers being uttered under a frightened breath. As we crossed the entrance of the fort, a calm came over me, the calm of a place of protection. I felt compelled to go inside the round turret at the corner of the fort, but rubble from walls that have collapsed over time blocked the entryway.

My friend's reaction was quite the opposite. She said her scalp crawled, and although the temperature was quite warm, goose bumps covered her arms. This reaction continued the entire time we were at the Real Presidio de San Sabá. Even after we left, the sensations she experienced remained with her for the next ten to twelve miles.

We made several other stops and passed the Real Presidio de San Sabá on our return route. Her bad feelings, along with the goose bumps, returned until we were well away from Real Presidio de San Sabá. She only has to speak about the presidio and the same goose bumps and other ill feelings return to her.

The turret at the Real Presidio de San Sabá stands as a reminder of
the Spanish explorers who brought life to this part of Texas.
WIKIMEDIA COMMONS

I believe that the urgency for me to go inside the tower came
from Fray Molina and his desperate prayers that remain, trapped
forever, inside the fallen presidio. I believe that in the midst of
those ruins, all who venture into the Real Presidio de San Sabá
will fall under the protection of Fray Molina's prayers.

We were told that on nights when the Comanche Moon rides
high in the sky, Fray Molina's whispered prayers and the clicking
of his rosary are heard throughout the encampment.

For your own look at the Real Presidio de San Sabá, where a
replica of the frontier fort stands, drive one mile west of Menard,
Texas, on US Highway 190. The original fort was founded in 1757
and was operated by the Colonial Spanish Army until abandoned
in 1772 by order of the Viceroy of New Spain.

There is no admission charge and visitors are welcome to take self-guided tours 365 days a year. Group tours are available with advance notice. The county golf course is located next door to the presidio.

Several archaeological digs have been conducted at this historic site, and it has undergone significant restoration work. Real Presidio de San Sabá was chosen as the site of the 2003 Texas Archeological Society Field School. Volunteer excavators from across the state convened in June of that year to work alongside Texas Tech students. The site includes a covered pavilion with restroom facilities. Enjoy a picnic lunch or dinner on-site and take in the beautiful surroundings while pondering what life would have been like as a Spanish soldier on the frontier!

PART II

FORTS ESTABLISHED BETWEEN 1800 AND 1845

FORT ANAHUAC

Col. Juan Davis Bradburn, a Kentuckian serving in the Mexican army, sat back in his chair and closed his eyes. Holding his riding crop in both hands, he gently rubbed his brow with the leather-bound whip and listened to the outrageous lies of the colonists' leader.

"Sir, are you listening to me?" Col. William B. Travis slammed his fist on Colonel Bradburn's desk.

Sleepily opening his eyes, Bradburn stared at the Texan.

"These things you are saying are lies, my friend. It is against the Mexican laws for you and your companions to come in here making these false accusations without proof."

"A young woman's virtue was taken against her will and you want more proof!" Travis shouted.

"Her word against the word of my men? I am not going to believe an Anglo woman over my men. They were only doing their duty." Bradburn stood and walked to the window. He looked out at the compound and then turned back to the men in the room.

"My troops say the young wench begged them to take her, so her father and brother wouldn't have to pay the collections I sent my men to get from them. I do not call that against her will. If she offered her, shall we say, treasures, she deserves what she received."

Colonel Bradburn frowned and pointed to the door. "Now get out of here, I have work to do."

Travis knew he wasn't getting anywhere and, trying to be businesslike, stood for a few moments thinking. Frustrated by Colonel Bradburn's obvious disregard for his protests, Travis held his ground.

"I will not leave until I've had satisfaction in this matter."

"Don't try my patience, Mr. Travis. I am a busy man and I don't have time for your complaints." Bradburn turned to leave the room. Travis grabbed the colonel's arm and spun the smaller man around.

"How dare you touch me? Guard! Guard!"

Quickly, Travis and the men with him were surrounded with rifles pointed at them.

"Let this pack of rabble-rousers cool their tempers in our stockade for a while, at least until I decide what to do with them. They will work like the rest of the convicts. Perhaps building a Mexican garrison will change their attitudes for the better."

Bradburn smiled as his guards led William Travis, Munroe Edwards, Patrick C. Jack, and several others to the old wooden barracks.

Shortly after the men were incarcerated, Col. Francis White Johnson received a message telling him of Travis's wrongful capture. Johnson dispatched a letter to Bradburn demanding the release of the Texans. Bradburn scoffed at the demands, and subsequently troops were assembled and the fighting began.

The Fort Anahuac stockade was first established militarily in November 1830. It was to be a garrison to protect against Anglo-American colonization, to collect customs duties in Texas, and to enforce a Mexican law passed on April 6, 1830.

Fort Anahuac was a short-lived outpost. The capture and subsequent release of William B. Travis and his volunteers in 1832 saw most of the fort dismantled by Texas troops. Four months after Colonel Travis's release, in November, a fire gutted the wooden sections of the fort. Ultimately, in December, the stockade where Travis and his men were unjustly held burned to the ground. Settlers of the area did not allow the good stone fireplaces and chimneys to go to waste. They carried them away one stone at a time for use in their own homes, leaving nothing but ruins behind.

When Mexican troops tried to reopen the fort in 1835, they ordered lumber to be shipped in for the rebuilding of Fort Anahuac. Outraged Texans, including William Barret Travis, burned the lumber before it ever reached Anahuac, forcing the Mexican troops, who had no artillery, to hide in the woods and leave the area forever. Fort Anahuac was never reopened.

The story of Col. William Barret Travis and his unjust imprisonment began in 1832. On June 10, 1832, William B. Travis and his volunteers' rebel yells were heard amidst the gunfire and confusion in the Spanish fort where much blood was shed. Two days later, the battle ended, but a war was just beginning. The war for Texas's independence from Mexican reign had begun and sparked the fighting at Fort Velasco and the adoption of the Turtle Bayou Resolutions. The confrontation with Travis and the Texans resulted in Bradburn's and the Mexican troops' removal from the post.

The shots fired that fateful day, in the old stockade more than a hundred years ago, started a movement to free all men wrongly imprisoned. The ghosts of some of those men seem to be imprisoned still—and some claim to have seen the ghost of Colonel Johnson riding up on a great black stallion to set his men free.

On hot summer mornings, after a downpour the night before, a gray blanket of mist seems to cover the earth. On such mornings, visitors of the Fort Anahuac Park may witness the reincarnation of one of the most stunning scenes in Texas, as out of the fog emerges a pale figure that some say could be Col. Francis White Johnson. He rides a great black stallion along what was once Fort Anahuac's perimeter, toward what appears to be a wooden building. There he

State marker at Fort Anahuac

reaches for a pistol and shoots the lock off the massive door. William Barret Travis and others rush out into the mist and disappear. Perhaps while you visit Fort Anahuac, you could see the same.

The last remaining fort wall succumbed to the rechanneling of the Trinity River when it collapsed into the water. Today, Fort Anahuac Park offers a boat ramp, a wooden fishing pier, and a children's playground. Preliminary archeological excavations at Anahuac have been carried out, and plans for a full-scale excavation and the construction of an interpretive museum are included in this historic site's future.

A few exposed ruins and a historical marker are all that remain of Fort Anahuac, located on State Highway 564 one mile south of Anahuac in the Chambers County Park.

FORT BEND

Fort Bend, a rather small compound, was established in November 1822. It was built on the location selected by Stephen F. Austin because it was on the most favorable ford of the Brazos River. The blockhouse was the first building erected at Fort Bend.

Fort Bend became important to the Texas Revolution because the rear guard detachment defended the crossing against Mexican invasion. Wiley Martin was commander of the rear guard. He was outmaneuvered by General Santa Anna and forced to transport some of his troops across the Brazos at the crossing. After Santa Anna's defeat at San Jacinto, the Texans used the small fort briefly.

The troops led by Thomas Jefferson Green stopped and rested for a few days at Fort Bend before pressing onward in pursuit of the Mexican army. A little-known Colonel George was left in command of a handful of troops to protect the settlers.

Corp. Frank Ashton, a farmer's son under the command of Colonel George, fell in love with the colonel's daughter, Nancy. Frank broke off with a local girl, Anna Barber, who claimed she was in love with him. After he told Anna he was going to marry the colonel's daughter, she threatened to kill the two of them and herself. Frank shrugged off the threats as hollow and asked the colonel for Nancy's hand in marriage. The colonel refused his request and would not allow them to see each other under any circumstance.

The couple began sneaking off to nearby Richmond to be in each other's arms. Frank built a two-story house near the fort and furnished it with care. He bought only what Nancy wanted for the house. She visited at every chance, decorating the inside and planting a flower garden.

Frank tended to his duties at Fort Bend and came home at night to an empty house, except for the smell of Nancy's lilac water lingering in the air. He hardly ever saw Nancy except at the fort when he'd catch a glimpse of her or on those special occasions when she would sneak to the house on the days he wasn't on duty.

One evening when he came home from the fort, Nancy met him at the door crying. He consoled her while she sobbed about a fight she had with her father. They spent the night holding each other.

Neither of them had any idea they were being watched; they were oblivious to the fate awaiting them. While they slept curled in each other's arms, Anna slipped into the house and murdered them, then turned the gun on herself.

As I interviewed the folks in the area, I was told about Frank and Nancy. I was also told about the late John List and his experiences at the Ashton house.

John List was a native of Fort Bend County, and he worked for a local real estate office in Richmond, Texas. His story was told to me by his nephew, who once listened at his uncle's knees about the ghosts of the Ashton house near where Fort Bend once stood.

"He said he hesitated as he unlocked the door to Frank Ashton's house. His agency had been selected to sell the old house more than once, and each time something went wrong with the sale. Most of the time potential buyers were frightened away by strange voices and incidents going on in the house. Being the top seller for the company, Uncle John had decided that he wanted to take a shot at selling the house this time around.

"The first time he went in the house alone to take inventory for the ad description, nothing out of the ordinary occurred," the nephew told me. "When the ad about the house came out in the local newspapers, Uncle John received several calls the first morning, and one couple made arrangements to look at the house.

"Uncle John often told us that when he and the prospective buyers entered the house, odd things immediately started happening. The screams the lady customer let out when a light started flashing off and on were nothing compared to the horrified look on her face when the burners on the stove flared to life. Even her husband didn't have a logical explanation for the footsteps in the upstairs hallway. Uncle John said those footsteps echoed all through that big old house." Chuckling, the nephew continued, "Knowing there shouldn't be anyone except the three of them in the house, Uncle John left the customers in the foyer and started up the stairs to take a look merely to satisfy his own curiosity. He heard a girl giggling. He found no one, but the giggling never stopped. Uncle John and the young couple started down the sidewalk, and each turned back to see if they could see who was giggling and whispering. He told us that the sounds were a whole lot like those made by children playing tag on hardwood floors.

"Uncle John said he showed the house to twenty-seven potential buyers. They each came once and never returned. When he contacted the owners of the beautiful old home, he found out the family knew about the ghosts all along.

"He said that Mr. Ashton wasn't shocked at all when he was told there was a problem with the house. He just sighed and told John that if the agency couldn't sell the house, they would do something else with it.

"Well, Uncle John asked him if there was anything he could tell him about the history of the house. Then he told Mr. Ashton about eerie things that kept happening every time he took prospective buyers to the house. He said everybody loved the house until the shenanigans started, and most folks didn't stay around. Not one of the customers he showed the house to ever viewed the upstairs rooms.

"Uncle John said that was when Mr. Ashton told him he and his brother didn't really want to but they would just have to tear the house down since it was obviously haunted. He said they had known about the ghosts for a long time, and they had a family meeting and made that decision. He told Uncle John that his phone call had confirmed what they needed to do, and he thanked Uncle John for trying."

The house Frank built had been passed from one niece or nephew to the next and had come on the market many times. Laughter and footsteps continued to echo through its walls regardless of who owned it. None of the folks who considered buying the house ever advanced past the ghostly lovers' games.

According to John List's nephew, the lovers are rumored to be roaming free now, chasing each other through other vacant houses in the area, giggling and carrying on as if they were children playing a game. Long before the house was torn down, old-timers told of seeing shadows in the upstairs rooms when moonbeams filtered through the vacant windows. Frank and Nancy roamed from room to room, arm in arm, enjoying their newfound freedom.

Fort Bend's name was given to the county when it was established in 1837. Soon the smaller Fort Bend area was swallowed up by nearby Richmond when it was selected for the county seat. The Texas Centennial Commission erected a monument to Fort Bend because of its role in the revolution.

If you would like to visit the site, the best way is to go to Fort Bend, Texas, and visit the historical museum there.

WOODS' FORT

Stopping for an evening snack at a roadside park in Fayette County, my friend and I thought we heard a bell ringing in the distance.

We crossed the barbed-wire fence and headed out across an open field to see where the noise was coming from. Reaching a stand of trees, my friend turned to me. "What are you laughing at?"

"I wasn't laughing. What's the matter with you?"

"Now, don't tell me that. I heard you laughing. Don't try to scare me that way. You know I'm not easy to scare."

"Wasn't me, Sammy. Come on, there's no one out here ringing a bell. Must have been on a cow or a goat or something." I started back to the park area with Sammy close by.

Weird laughter exploded, echoing across the meadow. We bolted, fear propelling us toward the fence. When I tried to jump over the fence, one of the barbs caught my pants leg. Sammy glanced first at me and then at the truck.

"Sammy, don't you even think about it. Get me off this fence. Don't you leave me here!"

Sammy reluctantly returned and we both tugged, I at my pants while Sammy yanked on my arm. Eerie laughter continued to fill the hot afternoon air.

"Tear them if you have to, EC, and let's get out of here. We can buy another pair when we get back to town. Just get loose from it and let's get out of here."

"Can't you see I'm trying?" I yanked my leg over the fence, ripping a hole in my new pants. I sprinted to the pickup and jumped behind the wheel.

Sammy slid into the passenger seat, and we smoked out of there, leaving our drinks and picnic lunch on the concrete table. The laughter followed us for several miles.

"Don't know who was doing all that laughing, but they must really be proud of themselves. They scared the daylights out of me." Sammy squirmed in her seat.

I assumed a calm demeanor, one I was far from feeling. "Woods' Fort once stood out there in that field. I'll bet it was some ghosts we heard." Sammy turned in the seat and looked back at the roadside park.

"Well, that is what we came to do—see if there were any ghosts out there. Should we go back and investigate further?" I was willing to return to the roadside park.

"No, thank you. We know there are ghosts around these old fort sites, and what we heard today confirms it. You can just do some research and find out who it might have been; that place gave me the heebie-jeebies."

We drove on and later, when I returned home and thought more about it, I regretted not staying around to investigate further, but I did my research and found out about Lem and Ace, who worked at Woods' Fort. An officer in the War of 1812, Zadock Woods, moved to Texas and built his compound to offer protection from Indian attacks to the colonists who settled the vicinity.

Lem Creech and Ace Harper had drifted into the area and often visited the compound for days at a time. They worked for "old man Woods" as they called him, when they weren't playing jokes on folks.

In 1838 Ace and Lem ran into the stronghold of Zadock Woods yelling, "Indians are attacking!"

The cook for the single men at the compound shook his finger at the two men. "Lem, you and Ace just as well forget about your practical jokes. We've decided not to fall for any more of your shenanigans."

Lem and Ace always got a kick out of seeing their coworkers jump to the ready, waiting for an attack. Their laughter would ring out across the fortified compound, but today was a disappointment to them.

Seeing that none of the men were going to take the bait, Ace poured himself a cup of coffee. Lem watched his friend as most of the other men left the bunkhouse.

"Now, you boys better listen to us and get those settlers in here and out of the fields, afore them Injuns gets too close."

"They was riding fast and about a half-mile ahead of their dust. Weren't they, Lem?"

"Sure was, Ace." Lem held up his cup.

Ace never was a man to give up on an idea. Lem studied his partner and grinned. Boy, he was a convincing son-of-a-gun when he set his mind to it, which was most of the time.

He watched Ace strut around the low-ceilinged structure. Hitching up his britches a notch, he prodded at the men left inside. "I tell you there's an Injun attack coming and it won't be long." Turning, he winked at Lem. "Right, Lem?"

"Sure enough, Ace. They'll be here afore we know what happened. You'd better listen to him, fellers. We saw their dust." Lem sipped his hot coffee, enjoying the show Ace was putting on at the other end of the room. Waving Lem and Ace off, the others went about their work.

"These boys are no fun anymore, Lem," Ace complained quietly. "We just as well get on out of here. I don't even like working here anymore. The pay's getting a little slim for all Old Zadock has us a doin' lately. He just wants more and more work."

"I'm with you, Ace. Let's head out." Lem watched as Ace picked up his extra shirt and pants and stuffed them into his saddlebags. "I'll get our horses saddled."

"All right, you go on and do that, and I'll go talk to old man Woods. I think we can find friendlier folks down the road." Ace continued stuffing his saddlebags with coffee beans and hardtack from the larder in the corner. "Here, put this in your bags." Ace tossed Lem a coffeepot as he started out the door, saying, "I ain't got room for it."

Lem rode up to the main house while leading Ace's horse and saw Ace talking to Colonel Woods on the porch. "You leaving so soon, boys?"

"We just gotta move on, Mr. Woods. You understand, don't you? Things are getting a bit too crowded here now."

"Sure I do, boys. If you ever need a job and you're in the area, just look me up."

After drawing their wages, Lem and Ace left the Woods' Fort compound. They rode a few hours before making camp for the night.

"This looks like a good spot for a camp. Water's not too far off, and it's pretty well protected." Lem took inventory of their surroundings. The running creek curved around a stand of trees nearby, and the mesquite brush was too short for any Indians to hide behind. He glanced at Ace as he dismounted and pulled the saddle off his horse.

"Here Lem, take the horses down to the creek and give them a drink then stake them over there in that stand of saplings. I'll get us a fire going and see what we might have to cook up for supper."

Lem unsaddled his mount. He led the horses to the creek and then hobbled them in the tall prairie grass near the young trees.

"Ace, don't you think you built the fire too big?"

"It has to be big to keep all the coyotes away. Got some beans and bacon for supper, unless you feel lucky enough to shoot a rabbit or something before it gets too dark."

"Nah, beans and bacon are good for me tonight. My backside is pretty tired right about now. I think I'll just sit right here on this nice soft grass and relax a little bit."

"Lem, I swear if you ain't getting plumb lazy."

"No lazier than you, my friend. You wouldn't even tether your own horse tonight."

"Lem, what you so touchy about?"

"Ah, nothing, 'ceptin' I was getting pretty used to sleeping on a nice soft bed under a nice warm roof there at the fort."

"Yep, me too." Ace handed his friend a plate of beans and bacon and poured him a cup of thick dark coffee. When they finished cleaning up the dishes, they sat and smoked their pipes for a little while before Lem started yawning.

"About that time, ain't it, Ace?"

"Yep, been a long day. Let's turn in." Rolling into their blankets near the fire, they slept part of the night in quiet peace until a strange night bird called out sharply.

Ace sat up abruptly. "What was that, Lem?"

"Ain't sure, Ace, but I think we'd better get back to the compound. What do you think? I don't rightly like the idea of being out here all alone."

Pulling on his boots, Ace kicked dirt over the burned-down campfire. "Yep, I think that'd be a good idea, Lem. You get the horses and I'll pack this stuff up."

Saddling the horses, Lem led them back to where Ace stood waiting with the bags bulging. Lem noticed a strange expression in Ace's eyes.

"What's the matter with you, Ace?"

"It's Injuns, Lem. I saw one of 'um running out of the brush. I'll bet they was after the horses."

"We'd better git pretty darned quick then."

Their horses saddled, Lem and Ace rode back to just outside the gates of Woods' Fort and started ringing the warning bell for Indian attacks. After two strikes of the metal triangle, both men slumped to the ground, shot in the back with flaming arrows.

Alerted to possible danger, the settlers gathered around the inside perimeter of the compound, where they fought for several hours before the Indians gave up and rode away. The men had held off the attack without losing any lives inside the fort. If Lem and Ace hadn't come back to warn them, the settlers could have been wiped out easily. The Kiowas had meant to attack while the settlers inside Woods' Fort slept.

Nowadays, Lem and Ace roam the vicinity of Woods' Fort, watching and waiting for some unsuspecting soul to stop at the nearby roadside park so they can play their practical jokes. A historical marker about the fort was erected in 1936 at a location a mile and a half west of West Point on State Highway 71 at its junction with County Road 117. It reads: "In 1828–1842, the fortified residence of Zadock Woods, veteran of the War of 1812, was used by colonists of this vicinity as a protection against Indian attacks. One of the old 'Three Hundred' of Austin's colonists, he was the oldest man killed in the 'Dawson Massacre' September 18, 1842."

There was also another historical marker at this site, but it was stolen in 1986, according to information in the Fayette Heritage Museum & Archives.

The roadside park has changed considerably since our visit that day; it now has a rock barrier instead of a barbed-wire fence. I wonder if the folks who visit the same park now ever hear the same laughter of the spirits we heard.

FORT BIRD

After the battle of Village Creek in May 1841, Maj. Jonathan Bird led the expedition that would lend protection to settlers in the area against marauding Comanches and Wichitas. Clouds rolled in from the northwest behind the company of cavalry officers and troops who came to establish Fort Bird in October 1841. The fort consisted of a blockhouse and several smaller buildings enclosed by a picket stockade.

Bird's soldiers and Capt. Alexander Webb's men occupied the stockade until March 1842. In September of that year, the fortress housed a special council between nine Indian tribes and representatives of the Republic of Texas. Later it became known as Birdville in Tarrant County.

It was early in 1842 when a lone rider came into the small camp that sprang up on the outskirts of Fort Bird. Simpson Trask stood in the makeshift saloon and boasted of killing a hundred or more Indians in his travels.

"I tell you men, I'm the best there is when it comes to taking care of your Indian troubles. I can scalp a red-skinned rascal in two minutes flat and still have time to show women how a man can really love a lady." He tugged at Beth Ann, one of the working girls at the saloon.

He kissed her cheek and whispered to her, and she giggled like a young schoolgirl. He slapped her on the behind, and she walked to the other end of the room to wait for him.

Simpson bragged about killing the chief of a small band of Wichitas. He was explicit in his description of making the chief watch as his wife and daughter were molested and killed. The men at the Fort Bend saloon sat trying to ignore the voice of the braggart, and some began to leave. Eventually Simpson took Beth Ann to her pleasure tent in back of the saloon. The men who'd remained breathed a sigh of relief when they watched Simpson go. They continued to pass the time in quiet, idly playing cards, smoking, and drinking.

Suddenly a scream of terror rent the air, causing all in the saloon to jump into action, running for the person in distress. The first to arrive on the scene of the crime was met with a gruesome sight.

Simpson lay dead on the floor of the tent, arrows protruding from his throat and chest. Other parts of his anatomy lay strewn about in a haphazard array. His scalp had been ripped from his head and his skull busted. His brains spilled out on the rug, blood soaking through it into the dirt floor.

Beth Ann sat with her knees pulled up to her chin, wide-eyed, shaking uncontrollably. Horrible bruises, purple and blue on her face, showed prominently in the dim lamplight. Her eyes were nearly swollen shut.

When questioned, Beth Ann mumbled only a few words while shaking her head and sobbing softly. "A ghost. War paint and feathers. Killed him."

Major Bird rushed into the tent just in time to see several men carrying Simpson's body outside. "What's going on out here?"

"This lady was entertaining this man and somebody broke in on them and well, sir, they killed him then mutilated his body pretty bad."

"Well, Sergeant, who was it?"

"That's just it, sir, the girl just mumbles something about ghosts and feathers and war paint."

"Who was the man who was killed?"

"Simpson is all we know, Major. He came in here this morning." The sergeant related the events from the time Simpson rode into the fort.

Major Bird shook his head. "Renegade. His kind will keep us all from ever settling this land. Keeping the Indians up in arms all the time. Bury him and turn in your report, Sergeant. As soon as the woman remembers or can tell you what happened, I want to be informed."

"Yes, sir."

A work detail buried Simpson's body without ceremony outside the fort. No marker was ever placed at the grave to show who he was or that he even existed.

For weeks afterward Beth Ann sat shocked and terrified at what she had witnessed. Months later, while talking to a friend, she related the story of the fearful night.

"Simpson was beating me in the face when suddenly a bright light appeared through the flaps at the end of the tent. Simpson was sitting on top of me, calling me names and hitting me in the face. He told me if I cried out, he would slit my throat and take me anyway.

"At first, I couldn't see what was going on, but he got really still, and when his eyes bugged out and blood dripped from his throat onto me, I screamed for help. The light behind the man turned into some kind of human figure. You know it looked like an Indian. First it was a light, then it was an Indian. His face was a gruesome twist of anger and paint all mixed together with bloody bruises." Beth Ann stopped for a moment to catch her breath.

"He had a couple of feathers sticking out from behind his headband. He looked like a chief. Arrows flew through the air and into Simpson's neck. The Indian then took a large knife and ripped off Simpson's scalp.

"The weird thing is the whole time neither the Indian nor Simpson made a sound. Only the gleam of terror in Simpson's eyes showed. He was scared plumb to death. If the Indian hadn't killed him outright, the man would have died from fright. The twisted revenge on that gruesome face was the only thing that showed." Beth Ann finished her story, and the two women cried together.

Some who know the legend feel that the ghostly Indian chief killed Simpson trying to protect Beth Ann because he was unable to protect his own wife and daughter from the same man. The ghost of the chief is believed to have appeared many times to help the working girls of local saloons. Even today, in our police-protected society, the chief appears when any woman in the area is molested and comes to her rescue.

In Arlington, seven miles to the south of what was Birdville, a stone marker commemorates Fort Bird. When my friend and I first visited Fort Bird, all visible remains were gone. In July 2006, work began to make a tourist attraction now called Bird's Fort Trail Park. Improvements include a Campión Trails Dedication Marker, a Campión Trails Gateway Monument, a concrete surface trail, eight tables under a large pavilion, plenty of parking, picnic areas, portable restrooms, a river overlook, shelters, walking trails, and two river overlook shelters.

FORT BOGGY

It was getting late in the day when my friend and I pulled up to the historical marker commemorating Fort Boggy's existence.

We stepped out of the car to stretch our legs and read the plaque about the time dusk began to fall. Soon the mystical figure of a young woman shrouded in light walked toward a grassy area that hadn't existed moments before. She sat underneath a gnarled oak that appeared near a dried-up creek bed. The woman sat staring into the empty stream, a look of contentment in her eyes. The sound of running water where none trickled eerily echoed through the air. Then we heard the woman's mournful cry wafting over the open fields around us.

When we arrived in the next town, we talked to several people about what we had seen and heard, and we were told that it was Martha Whitehead. She searches for her final resting place at dusk each night of the full moon.

We found out that at first Fort Boggy was actually a two-story blockhouse built in 1839. A company of Texas Rangers protected

37

the settlers of the area, and soon a settlement grew up around the fortress. The settlement sported a general store, a sawmill, and a doctor.

After being established near present-day Leona, Fort Boggy was fairly small and was often targeted for attack by the nomadic tribes of Comanches, Lipan Apaches, Kiowas, and other Indians in the area; however, it wasn't the Indians who finally ended Fort Boggy's usefulness.

Several attacks on the fort had started to take its toll on the settlers and their supplies. In the spring of 1841, a cholera epidemic nearly decimated the entire settlement.

Martha Whitehead, wife of Dr. Charles Whitehead, was a tremendous help to her husband. Working day and night, she nursed his patients, administered medications, and performed any other necessary nursing duties.

One afternoon Martha looked longingly out the window where the sunshine and blue skies beckoned. She removed her apron and turned to her husband. "Charles, I'm going for a walk down to the creek. I'll not be gone too long."

"Be careful, my dear. I couldn't do all I have to do without you here by my side." Charles Whitehead looked at his wife and pushed a stray curl off her forehead.

"I'll be fine, Charles." She rubbed her back and kissed him lightly on the cheek.

"Dr. Whitehead, we need you in here."

"Go on, Charles, I'll see you in a bit." Martha watched her husband walk away with one of the homesteaders.

She strolled down the path and settled under the beautiful old oak. She smiled, remembering the surprise Charles had sprung on her the day after they were married. When her husband told her they were moving to Texas, she was frightened, yet, loving him the way she did, she was determined to be a good wife. She followed without hesitation and helped him tirelessly.

Her only rest came when she could steal away to the old oak tree. She loved it because it brought her peace of mind to watch the water in the creek bed at the fort's entrance. The ground sloped downward from the land around it and overlooked a shallow running stream where the fort got its water supply. Martha loved the grassy area beneath the tree and somehow found a few moments each day to visit. Sitting there alone, she dreamed of her girlhood home and how she would like to return to see her parents.

She shared her special spot and her thoughts with no one except her husband.

A recent letter from her mother had told of a beautiful fall in Georgia. The flowers of autumn were blooming and the fragrances were strong on the muggy mornings. Her father had new horses to care for and he was happy, although they missed her dearly. She missed them likewise; still, her home was in Texas now.

Martha rubbed her temples to ease the pain in her head, hoping she wasn't coming down with an illness. Charles needed her now more than ever. Looking at the watch attached to the pin her mother had given her to wear on her bodice, she remembered she must return to her work.

The endless tasks of helping others finally took their toll. During the outbreak of cholera, Martha fell ill and, weakened from not enough rest due to helping others, she succumbed to the fever much quicker than most. She knew she would not survive, so she called her husband away from his other patients.

In the bedroom they had shared for the past couple of years, Martha lay in her bed, her skin hot and dry to the touch. The lamp on the table near the bed cast a sickly yellow hue across her face as her husband gently smoothed back her hair. Martha tried to reach up and take his hand but was too weak, and her hand fell back to the soft white sheets.

"Charles, I won't keep you more than a moment. I know how the others need you. Promise you'll bury me under the oak. I love it at the creek, and I love you, more than you will ever know." Martha closed her eyes and breathed her last.

"Yes, my love." Charles Whitehead bowed his head in sorrow. His beloved was gone from him forever.

The next morning, his heart heavy, Charles Whitehead ordered his wife's grave dug under the big oak tree. A scant half an hour later, the men digging the grave reported water to be continually seeping into the shallow grave they'd dug. It would be impossible to bury Mrs. Whitehead in her chosen spot. In his grief, Charles consented to have the men dig her grave elsewhere, and Martha was laid to rest on a knoll of land overlooking the oak and Fort Boggy. Charles hoped Martha would understand.

If you listen closely, you might hear Martha's mournful cry while she searches for her preferred resting place under the oak. At the time I visited the Fort Boggy area, the oak was gone and the stream was a bed of rocks with no water, but after a rain a muddy hole would appear near where my friend and I saw the oak tree and Martha's ghost.

By 1941, nothing remained of the old fort except the Texas Centennial Commission's marker at the site of Fort Boggy in Leon County, near present-day Leona. In 2001, Fort Boggy State Park was opened and it encompasses 1,847 acres in Leon County. The land was donated sixteen years earlier to the Texas Parks and Wildlife Department by Eileen Crain Sullivan, the widow of prominent Centerville banker Joe Sullivan. The Sullivan family's roots in the county date from 1860.

Visitors who explore the park shouldn't expect to find remains of its namesake, Fort Boggy. It was a palisaded fort constructed in the area in 1840 and named for a nearby creek. The exact location for the garrison is pretty much unknown except for a written account of the area's history. It is said that the seventy-five-square-yard fort consisted of two blockhouses and eleven dwellings, and it sheltered approximately seventy-five residents seeking refuge from Indian raids. Both the Keechi and the Kickapoo tribes inhabited the region at that time.

The Sullivan family dug a fifteen-acre lake over a century later after the fort was constructed, in 1940. Today, the lake remains un-named but is the park's focal point. It attracts waterfowl and wildlife, as well as recreation-seekers.

The park's location, midway between Dallas and Houston, and its closeness to Interstate 45 make it a popular hot spot for friends and families who live in North and southeast Texas. According to some of the locals, Fort Boggy is the best-kept secret in central East Texas.

MOORE'S FORT

Moore's Fort was a twin blockhouse built in 1826 by John Henry Moore near what is now Round Top, Texas. It was originally located where La Grange, Texas, is today. The fort was built for his family and the nearby settlers' protection. It was later moved to Round Top for restoration. A historical marker sits at the original site of the fort.

At that time in Texas, many lawless men traveled to the area to seek livelihoods with few restrictions and the native Indians of the area were at war with the settlers who came to take their lands.

In the early 1800s it was common practice for white men to capture Indian women and keep them for their own pleasures as well as to cook and clean for them. Afterward, when the white man was no longer interested in her, the Indian woman would be left to her own devices to live the rest of her life in seclusion, rejected by her own people.

Jake Stevens often scouted for the army. He was a violent man who made his home outside the fort in a small cabin he built for himself. After a rather long scouting trip for the army, Jake captured an Indian girl, Little Turtle, the daughter of a Comanche tribal shaman.

Jake took his frustrations out on the Indian girl and apparently enjoyed her suffering immensely. It was not out of the ordinary to hear screams of pain and terror coming from Jake's cabin. Many times Jake was seen leaving the compound of Fort Moore carrying a jug of whiskey with him.

Later he could be heard shouting obscenities at Little Turtle. When the shouting subsided, the crack of a whip, followed by more cries of pain, could be heard.

Many times the guards at their posts saw the young Indian woman running away from the long black whip Jake wielded. She was never seen except on such occasions. Jake didn't allow her out of the cabin except to gather wood or take care of outdoor chores.

One especially violent night, Jake burst through the door of his cabin in a drunken rage.

"Woman, where are you?"

Little Turtle peeped out from behind the curtain hanging over the pantry closet. Meekly she walked out with her hands full of meat to add to the stew bubbling over the fire.

"I thought I told you to have my supper ready when I come through that door." Jake hefted the whiskey jug to his mouth and swilled down the liquor.

"Yes, supper ready." Little Turtle dipped up a large plate of stew from another pot on the hearth. "You eat now." Setting the plate in front of him, she stepped around behind Jake to get the bread off the shelf above the fireplace.

"Get over there and sit down." He grabbed her wrist and flung her down on the pallet in the corner of the room.

She sat quietly with her gaze on the floor. Tonight would be the night of no return. She would no longer endure his beatings and hurtful ways. Her people would not take her back, but she could survive.

"What is it you're a scheming about behind those evil black eyes?" Jake yelled, standing over her.

She only shook her head in answer to his question. Little Turtle had felt the long black whip many times, but she would no longer take his abuse. She would leave after he slept from the drink he brought home.

"Stand up and look at me when I ask you something. What are you planning?" He grabbed her braids and yanked her to her feet, forcing her to look into his eyes. "You better not even think about leaving here. I'll kill you first."

When she blinked, Jake slapped her hard on the jaw, sending her sprawling to the floor.

"Now get up. Get back over here." He unbuckled his belt. Little Turtle looked at him, and then darted for the door.

Once outside, she ran for the trees and fell on her knees to scoot under the brush. Jake staggered after her, arcing and cracking his long black whip.

"You'd better get on back out here where I can see you, girl. I ain't one to air dirty laundry in front of the whole world, but I will if I have to. You know that."

Little Turtle heard Jake shouting at her; then she looked up at the blockhouse where the soldiers stood watching him. Tonight Jake would get what was coming to him. She had waited as long as she could. She had gathered the herbs for a powerful medicine bag and hung it around her neck that morning. Jake couldn't hurt her anymore.

Little Turtle peered out from the underbrush where she held her breath. He mustn't find her before she was ready. She caressed the bone handle of the knife in her hand, rolling it from side to side. Her father had taught her to make weapons and the words to say as she worked. The spirit world could make a weapon either weak or invincible. The powers of a medicine man were many, and as the only child of a Comanche shaman, Little Turtle learned much from her father.

Jake beat the tops of the brush, yelling and screaming for her to come out, but she continued to wait. When he passed her by, Little Turtle breathed a sigh of relief barely audible.

"Get on out here, you little wench, I'm not finished with you." Little Turtle edged out from the brush behind Jake and stalked him. She darted from tree to tree, wishing he would get to the point she had chosen earlier. It would be to her best advantage to wait, but deep inside her, the anticipation built. Anxiety tried to take control of her senses, but she bided her time. He was headed straight for the trap she would spring on him. Sweat dripped between her eyes, and she licked her lips with expectation. Little Turtle stopped abruptly. She watched as Jake stepped into the circle of rope covered with leaves. Swiftly, her knife fell against the rope holding the sapling to the ground, and Jake's huge body flew through the air, his screams of anger cutting through the darkness. Briefly, Little Turtle stood motionless. What if the soldiers came to see what was the matter with the white man? No, they didn't like Jake any better than she did, so that was not likely. She stood in front of the dangling man and listened to his demands for release and smiled.

Spitting at him, she held the knife out for his inspection. The fear in his eyes told her what she wanted to know. Little Turtle tossed the knife just out of his reach and snatched up the black whip from the ground. She uncoiled and cracked the long leather snakelike bullwhacker.

"Now, little girl, you ain't aiming to whip old Jake, are you? I been good to you. I fed you and kept clothes on your back. I took you out of the filthy village you lived in and gave you a home with civilized folks. You ain't aiming to hurt old Jake, are you? Cut me down from here and we'll go on home and have a nice supper, just the two of us. What do you say?"

The tone of his voice made Little Turtle smile. He was afraid, just like she had been. That was good. He should be afraid. He would never see the light of another day.

"Get me down from here! I am losing my patience with you, girl. You cut those ropes and let me down right now."

Little Turtle cracked the whip across Jake's back again and again. Her pent-up anger released, she cried harder with each blow to his body. His shirt hung in ribbons of blood and cloth. Blood ran in drying rivulets onto his face. His hoarse screams turned to moans of agony as he begged for mercy and then was silent.

The terror of what she had done seeped into Little Turtle's mind. If anyone found her here with the white man like this, they would kill her. It would make no difference that he deserved what she had dealt to him; the white man wouldn't ask questions first. Little Turtle threw the whip to the ground and reached for the knife and ran away. The darkness was dense, and she didn't see the log blocking her pathway. She tripped and fell headlong to the ground, impaling herself on the knife she carried. Little Turtle died facedown in the dirt, the way Jake had often left her after beating her senseless.

Sometimes at dusk, an Indian girl can be seen running toward a grove of trees. A large man with a whip coiled around his shoulder runs after her. Moments later she returns alone and fades into the countryside.

A Texas Centennial Commission's marker stands as a reminder that Moore's Fort once existed, along with the two ghostly figures said to still roam the area. To see where the fort once stood, drive to Monument Hill just south of La Grange off State Highway 77. The reconstructed Moore's Fort is in Round Top, Texas.

FORT LIPANTITLÁN

The Mexican army established Fort Lipantitlán around 1825 to restrict immigration into Texas. It was built on the site of a Lipan Apache Indian camping grounds and an old presidio, which existed around 1734, on the west bank of the Nueces River.

The soldiers built Fort Lipantitlán of local materials, earthen works lined with wooden rails or pickets.

In author John Linn's *Reminiscences of Fifty Years in Texas*, he commented that the fort was only fit "perhaps, for a second-rate hog pen."

The number of troops garrisoning the fort ranged from 120 to 80 men at times. It is doubtful, though, that Fort Lipantitlán ever saw a fully armed regiment, even after some permanent buildings were erected.

Records show the battle of Lipantitlán, fought and won by Texans against the Mexican forces on November 4, 1835, took only a force of about seventy men. The Texans abandoned Fort Lipantitlán after the victory, and the fort grew up in brush. However, it continued to be used by Mexican troops periodically until they were driven from the area in 1842.

During its usefulness as a fort, a camp was situated to the side of Fort Lipantitlán and possibly housed some three hundred settlers and army families. The camp had its own laws and carried them out separately from the army affairs at the fort.

My friend Sammy and I visited the area where Fort Lipantitlán once stood, and when we arrived we heard mournful cries of, "Have mercy on me, please" from a woman whose voice became weaker by the minute. Searching for the source of the sounds proved fruitless. After we left the fort site, we talked to some of the residents in the area, and they shed some light on those sorrowful cries.

One lonely evening in late 1839, a young woman walked the floors of her small cabin, waiting for her husband to return. Several hours passed and he still had not come home. In her worried state, she decided to try to find out where he spent the nighttime hours.

She saw her husband leaving a small cabin, and she knew the woman who lived in the house. Devastated after she found her own husband coming from the woman's house, Katie began to cry.

Turning to go back to her home, tears streaming down her face, she paused to knock on a friend's door.

"Aggie, I saw him coming out of Milly Marlow's cabin. Then I saw him lean down and kiss her." She cried on the older woman's shoulder.

"Hush, now, Katie. I'll take care of Milly." The older woman handed the young wife a cloth. "Dry your eyes and blow your nose. You get on back to your house and act like you don't know a thing. You hear me?"

"Yes, ma'am."

Katie went back to her house, and Aggie kept her promise. She dressed to go out and told her own husband she would be back shortly. Knocking on the doors of several of the neighbors, all of them about her age, Aggie gathered a good-size crowd of angry women. As they walked along the street, their anger grew.

"That woman should have been run out of town a long time ago!" one woman yelled.

"Yes, when she first came here, we should have made her leave. Her kind is not what we want in our midst," another cried. "We'll take care of her tonight and she'll never bother another woman's husband again. Tar and feather her, run her out on a rail!" The cries went out.

Upon reaching Milly Marlow's house, Aggie pounded on the door. "Let us in, harlot."

Milly cowered in her cabin. Dread gripped her insides and she shook with fear. What were they going to do to her?

"Go away. I don't have anything to say to any of you."

"Let us in or we will burn you out."

Milly hid in the back of the house trembling.

The ladies busted the door open and filled the house. "You can't hide. We will find you."

Holding her breath, Milly hoped they wouldn't find her, but her hopes were dashed when Aggie flung the closet door back and dragged her out.

"No, leave me alone. Get out of my house!" Milly cried.

"Milly Marlow, you are guilty of adultery, and we are here to pass sentence on you. How do you plead?"

Milly, mortified to even have the women in her house, tried to bluff her way out of the situation. She had known Steve's wife would eventually find out and she told him as much, but he kept coming back to her.

She remembered when she and her own husband had come to Fort Lipantitlán, she had found Steve, a man she knew from the past. The two had parted company some time before she had met and married Herbert, and when he died she turned to Steve for comfort. Now these women were accusing her of wrongdoing when Steve should have been taking equal amounts of the blame with her.

"It is none of your business what I do in my own house. Now get out of here, you bunch of busybody peahens!" Millie cried.

"We ain't leaving until we have satisfied ourselves you won't be toying with any more of our men. We've known for a long time what kind of woman you are, and we've overlooked it because we didn't want sweet young Katie hurt, but she saw you with her husband tonight, and now you're going to pay for your crime."

Aggie motioned for the other women to carry out the plan. The women wrestled Milly to the ground and bound and gagged her.

They carried her to a tree outside of the settlement and threw a rope over a low, strong branch. Dropping the looped end of the rope around Milly's neck, they tightened it up.

"If you have any last words to say, now's your chance, harlot," one woman told her.

"There is no room for your kind in our settlement. Are you going to leave, or do we finish this job here and now?"

"I'm not leaving, and if you hang me, it will be on your conscience forever," Milly defied the mob.

Each of the women leaned on the rope, pulling Milly off the ground. Her pleas for mercy carried on the slight breeze.

"Leave her there, tied to the tree," Aggie ordered. "It'll let anyone else who thinks about adultery know we won't tolerate any of that sort of behavior here."

Milly's body swung in the breeze until Steve came the next morning and cut her down. He buried Milly, and then he left Katie and Fort Lipantitlán, never to return. Milly's cries are still heard in the winds that blow across the land of Fort Lipantitlán.

Today the site of Fort Lipantitlán is a state park, and although none of the old buildings are intact, the memories and legends live on in northwestern Nueces County about three miles upstream from the old town of San Patricio. The state marker for Fort Lipantitlán reads:

On This Site Stood Fort Lipantitlán. Occupied in 1831 by soldiers of the Mexican army to prevent further Anglo-American colonization in Texas, it was captured November 4, 1835 by volunteers under Captain Ira Westover. It was unsuccessfully attacked June 7, 1842 by 700 men under Gen. Antonio Canales while defended by 192 men under General James Davis. Five acres of land surrounding the site of the Fort were generously donated to the State of Texas by the heirs of J. C. Bluntzer in 1937.

Today, the site itself covers about five acres of densely packed mesquite trees. An old cistern and remnants of a small fountain can be found in the center of a circular drive that runs through the site. A few feet west of the cistern is a small, half-buried concrete marker with the word "Lipantitlán." This marker is visible only after the grass and weeds are mowed. At one time there were several picnic tables on concrete slabs in the small park, but these are gone, except for a few of the concrete slabs. Several private residences are located near the site. This takes away any feeling of being away from civilization. Fort Lipantitlán continues its history as a forlorn outpost of Texas history.

FORT COLORADO

Fort Colorado, established in 1836, was known by several names in its lifetime: Coleman's Fort, Fort Coleman, Fort Houston, and finally Fort Colorado. Established on the banks of Walnut Creek near the Colorado River in what is now Travis County, the fort was an important post in the series of defenses from the San Antonio River to the Trinity.

Fort Colorado and its garrison of rangers helped quell the attacks by Indians on white settlers between 1837 and early 1838. Troops abandoned Fort Colorado in 1838, and the community that later grew up around it became the capital city of the state.

People in the area tell the story of the commander, Col. Robert M. Coleman. He watched through the foggy mist for the man who had met him each night for months. When Walks With Doves appeared, Coleman would go to the blockhouse and slowly climb the stairs. He stayed for hours at a time, talking to the old medicine man from the nearby Comanche tribe. He never allowed anyone else in the blockhouse, and he gave no explanation for his actions.

He knew his troops wondered what he was doing in the lookout and hoped none of the men had observed the medicine man's arrival. They wouldn't understand why he went there alone at night with the old man. He never climbed the stairs to look out in the daylight hours because of his fear of heights. Somehow the old man knew of this and insisted on the cover of darkness.

Early one morning, Coleman overheard a conversation between his corporal and several other troops.

"I think the old fellow has lost his mind," Corporal James spouted.

The troopers, including the sergeant, stood close around Corporal James. James whispered, "I bet he's talking to his poor dead wife."

The first sergeant spoke up. "It ain't nobody's business what the colonel's doing."

"Well, if he is talking things over with his dead wife, I sure as heck ain't gonna follow him out onto the prairie after no Injuns. Are you?"

"If he says, ride, by jove, you'll ride." The sergeant shook his fist at the corporal.

"I say we'd better get in contact with somebody who will take this command away from him. He spends more time up there talking to himself than he does to us men."

Corporal James was not a man to back down from an argument, and he had a good point, but no one would openly agree with him.

Coleman watched as Sergeant Henry glared at Corporal James. The sergeant scratched his head and walked out of the room, leaving the younger men staring after him.

Colonel Coleman stood in the shadows and thought about the men's doubts over his sanity. How could he tell them he was trying to arrange a peace treaty with the Indians behind the army's back? If he told them about the medicine man, they would probably ruin the whole thing. He'd just have to bide his time and let the situation play itself out.

Colonel Coleman talked to Walks With Doves several nights in a row and promised he'd not ride against the tribes. He wouldn't give orders or make plans to follow direct orders from Washington.

Shortly after a new set of commands came through, Sergeant Henry contacted Colonel Coleman's superiors by letter. He outlined what he knew and told them that Colonel Coleman was acting strangely. An investigation into Colonel Coleman's actions ensued, and he was ordered to relinquish his command to Maj. William H. Smith.

Coleman refused to release his command. He argued with his superiors about Smith's abilities to take command. He knew Smith would lead the troops against the Indians in the territory. Coleman asked that they put Capt. Micah Andrews in command if they were determined to take away his authority. Coleman had helped train Andrews and knew he would be a good, levelheaded commander.

When Coleman finished his letter to the authorities in Washington, he once again climbed the stairs to the blockhouse, where he stayed alone for several days, even having his meals sent to him.

Coleman held his command until January 1837, when Capt. Micah Andrews arrived at the fort, at which time Coleman came down from the blockhouse where he'd spent several weeks with the medicine man.

"Colonel, I'm sorry it came to this." Micah Andrews held out his hand to Coleman.

"Micah, come with me," said Coleman, "I must explain something to you. I think you need to meet someone."

Coleman led the new commanding officer to the blockhouse, where they climbed the steep stairway. "Walks With Doves, this is Micah Andrews. He will be talking with you now. The great fathers in Washington have other orders for me."

"So this is what you've been doing," said the captain. "Why didn't you just tell someone?"

The old medicine man spoke slowly, "Micah Andrews. Colonel is a good man. He understands our fears. He keeps secret for me."

"I will try to understand too, Walks With Doves," Micah replied.

Walks With Doves started down the steps of the blockhouse when he was seen by one of the troopers on guard.

"Indian in the compound!"

The cry went up and before Coleman or Andrews could stop the soldier, he shot and killed the Comanche shaman, undoing everything that Coleman had accomplished. Many people claim that the medicine man's ghost still comes to the area where Fort Colorado once stood; he's looking for someone to understand his people.

There are no remains of the fort. A state historical marker on the side of the road, two and one half miles northeast of the Montopolis Bridge in Austin, is the only reminder of Fort Colorado.

FORT PARKER

The Parker family from Crawford County, Illinois, came to Texas in 1833. After gaining permission to settle in the Texas territory, Daniel Parker organized those who wanted to travel to Texas, and they left Illinois in July. Daniel and the majority of his followers settled near Elkhart and built their church, the Pilgrim Baptist Church.

Other members of the family decided to settle farther west and built "Parker's Fort" near the Navasota River. John Parker and his three sons, Silas, James, and Benjamin, began clearing land for the fortified stockade in December 1834.

On May 19, 1836, Comanche Indians approached Fort Parker. Inside the walls of Fort Parker, tension filled the hearts of the women. Children, afraid to breathe, stood beside their mothers, waiting to see what would happen. The air on that bright May morning felt heavy and ominous. Benjamin Parker had been warned by his father, John, not to give the Indians passage into the fort and to keep the gate closed, but the Comanches were there expecting someone to come out and talk to them.

A light-skinned brave waved a white flag for the settlers to see. Cynthia Ann, Benjamin's daughter, watched as the expression on her father's face changed from worry to relief. However, she somehow knew it was a mistake. In a matter of seconds, he opened the gates and walked out toward the group of Indians. He came back quickly, smiling at the others gathered around the gate.

"They only want meat. They're hungry. We'll feed them and they'll leave."

Benjamin turned to his brother Silas. "Get a side of beef from the smokehouse and I'll take it to them. You stay here with the women and children."

Doing as he was told, Silas Parker returned from the smokehouse with the beef and shouldered it over to his brother.

Benjamin whispered to Silas, "Leave the gate open, just in case."

Nodding, Silas watched as his brother bravely carried the food to the Indians in the clearing. One of the braves took the beef while several others crowded around Benjamin.

Cynthia crept up behind her uncle and watched as the Comanche braves surrounded her father.

"Close the gates!" Benjamin shouted, just before the Comanches drove their arrows into his body.

A deafening roar filled the air as the settlers fired their rifles into the horde of savages.

The Indians broke through the gate, running their horses over several of the children. Cynthia Ann, having hidden at the end of her parents' cabin, listened to her aunt's screams when one brave grabbed the baby from her arms. Cynthia Ann saw the Comanche hold the tiny baby in one hand high above his head for a few seconds before he slammed the child to the ground at its mother's feet.

Fort Parker in Groesbeck, Texas, was the first home of Cynthia Ann Parker, who was captured and raised by Comanches.

Cynthia Ann yelled and cried as she ran out of her hiding place toward the painted Indian. Her small fists flailed at the brave's leg. He howled with laughter at her and then reached down and pulled her off the ground. He laid her across his horse's shoulders and carried her out of the compound. Within minutes five of Cynthia Ann's family members were killed. She and her brother and three others were taken captive to the Comanche camp, where she grew to womanhood.

Soon she adapted to the ways of the Comanche and later married Chief Peta Nocona. She bore him three children, the best known of which was Quanah Parker, the last great Comanche chief. Cynthia was nine years old when she was captured, and she lived with the Comanches for twenty-four years.

Tossing and turning, Cynthia Ann Parker cried in her sleep. Dreams of capture surfaced to alert her to trouble. Since living with the Comanches, she had grown to accept many beliefs, such as those of the spirit world.

Awakening from the horrible dream, Cynthia Ann realized that the shots she heard were not in a dream but were real, and her husband's village was under attack by the army.

Fear clutched her heart when she peered through the front of her teepee. She saw several hundred soldiers gallop from the trees and underbrush. The soldiers were firing at her people as they tried to flee from the guns and horses. Terrified, she watched as her husband fell from a soldier's bullet.

Cynthia stood in her tracks for only a moment before she sprang into action and snatched up her tiny child. Shushing the baby, she wrapped her buffalo robe around the two of them and split the deerskin on the back of the teepee so she could slip through. She hurried toward the brush.

Ranger Tom Kelliher caught a glimpse of a woman running for the trees and urged his horse in her direction. He reached down from his horse and grabbed Cynthia Ann by the arm. He lifted her kicking and screaming off the ground. Pulling her up behind the saddle, he brought her back to where the other women and children of the village waited for their fate to be determined by the soldiers.

"Here's another one. She was trying to escape. Want me to shoot her?"

Unceremoniously, he dumped her to the ground and shoved her toward the crowd of frightened women and weeping children.

Cynthia held her head high. She would shed no tears. She'd been in this situation before, a captive, but this time she was not a child. Now that her husband was dead, her son would someday be the chief of the Comanche tribes. She knew this and deep in her heart she was proud.

The commanding officer, Capt. Sul Ross, rode past the group and looked down from his horse into the blue eyes of Cynthia Ann, known by her Indian name, Naduah. Pointing to her, he barked an order to the sergeant in charge.

"Put that one on a horse. She is no Indian. Look at her eyes, you fool! She could be the Parker girl. I think we found her brother, too."

I recently visited the reconstructed version of Fort Parker and walked toward the gate where Benjamin Parker was said to have gone out to take beef to the Comanches. I began to feel strangely alert, as if something wrong was going on inside the compound. A sense of fear and anxiety clutched at my throat, but when I passed the gate, the feeling ceased.

A child's fears were evident especially at the back gate of Fort Parker. An oppressive feeling loomed between the last cabin and the blockhouse. The gate stood slightly open where the path led to the well. I listened closely and thought I heard the sound of a child wailing in the distance—perhaps crying for her lost parents.

I am not sure who is at this replica of Fort Parker, but I suspect it must be the spirit of Cynthia Ann Parker, the brave little girl who had to change her entire way of life because she had no choice.

The remaining twenty-one survivors of the raid on Fort Parker left and made their way to modern-day Palestine, Texas. When Cynthia Ann was returned to her family, she found it impossible to adapt. She died of a broken heart barely four months after the death of her daughter, Prairie Flower, yearning for her Indian family and their free way of life.

To reach Fort Parker, take State Highway 14 out of Groesbeck four miles north to Park Road 35. Wind down the narrow tree-covered lane for a short distance. Out of Mexia, Texas, turn west on Park Road 35 just south of the state park and drive one mile; you will find the park headquarters and the reconstructed Fort Parker.

The park is open Wednesday through Sunday from 9:00 a.m. to 5:00 p.m.; admission for ages twelve and older is two dollars; admission for children ages six to eleven is one dollar; children age five and younger get in for free. Park passes do not apply to visitors of the fort. Admissions taken are used to keep this valuable part of Texas history alive.

FORT MILAM

According to some visitors, if you find yourself along the highway near Fort Milam at night, don't be surprised if you see a strange light turn into a headless ghost carrying a cowboy hat. Farmers who have witnessed the strange light believe the apparition is searching for his assailants.

Fort Milam was originally called Fort Viesca and was built on the west bank of the Brazos River in 1834 to protect the settlers from hostile Indians. In December 1835 the fort was given a new name in honor of Benjamin R. Milam. It was built mainly for the protection of settlers around Robertson's community of Sarahville de Viesca. Robertson's colony was a handful of settlers and the community was named after Sarah Roberston and then Governor of Texas, Agustín Viesca. It had a short life span and was soon named Fort Milam. It was abandoned in March 1836 during the Runaway Scrape, better known as the evacuation by Texas residents fleeing the Mexican Army of Operations during the Texas Revolution. It began as a result of the Battle of the Alamo and ran through the decisive Battle of San Jacinto. The government of the new Republic of Texas and the civilian population fled the Mexican forces. The citizens of Texas disagreed with martial law of the Mexicans and the Mexicans disagreed with the Independence of the Texans. Sam Houston was mainly responsible. He was the commander-in-chief of the Provisional Army of Texas. He was to recruit and train a military force to defend the population against troops led by Santa Anna.

Later when settlers returned to the area, Capt. Edward Burleson and three ranger companies were garrisoned at the fort until the following fall. Col. Robert M. Coleman's rangers with Capt. Thomas H. Barron's battalion manned Fort Milam on October 1, 1836.

Troops from the fort were dispersed to build other forts in the area, including Little River Fort, Fort Fisher, and Fort Henderson in 1837. By late summer of 1837, ranger enlistment had begun to dwindle. Many men were needed to protect the settlers, and the rangers needed new recruits.

Frank Taylor traveled to Texas from his eastern Virginia home and even fought a few Indians on his way, but after his horse came up lame and he'd been on foot for several days, he began to feel as skittish as a rabbit with an owl flying overhead.

He stopped for the night and decided to run a cold camp again.

Since he'd left home to join the rangers, he had come to know what lonely really meant. All his life he'd been a people person, but then the woman who stole his heart had changed everything, and here he was, in the middle of nowhere, all alone.

Suzanna had run off with a traveling salesman and left him high and dry. So, instead of moping around his folk's farm, he decided to take advantage of his hunting skills and become a Texas Ranger.

He wrote a letter to Col. Edward Burleson, who was in charge of organizing companies of men to be rangers to garrison the forts in Texas, but he hadn't expected to ever get a reply. It didn't take long for Burleson to send an answer to Frank with orders to come to Fort Milam. The letter he received warned Frank to be watchful of the Comanches who were constantly raiding the area.

Frank considered he was less than a day's ride to the fort. He hoped his horse was healed enough for him to ride.

He hadn't given much conscious thought to Suzanna since the night she'd broken his heart because he was too busy watching for Indians. Nevertheless, she was there in the back of his mind. It was like she'd never left him, and thoughts of her niggled away at him from afar.

"You know, Pike, you're not a bad horse at all," he whispered. "You went lame on me, but you don't nag and you don't fuss about where I take you or what you have to eat." Frank patted the horse's neck. "I think you're much better to have around than any danged ol' girl anyway."

The old horse nickered softly at Frank.

Patting the horse's nose, Frank bundled up against the winter night in his blanket and rested his head on the saddle. He gazed up at the stars. He was becoming accustomed to sleeping out of doors, and he kind of liked it. Maybe when he joined up with Colonel Burleson and the other new rangers, he could sleep with old Pike nearby out under the open skies.

He pulled his blanket tighter against a gust of moist air. "Well, on second thought, I might sleep indoors during the winter, Pike." The horse snuffled against Frank's ear and nudged him slightly. Drifting off to sleep, Frank dreamed of riding for the rangers instead of dreaming about Suzanna for the first time since he'd met her.

The next morning, he built a sputtering fire for making coffee and then started on his way early. Fort Milam shouldn't be too far, he thought, smiling. For the first time in weeks, Frank felt good about his decision to join the rangers. Within sight of the fort, Frank halted Pike and stared out across the beautiful scenery. Taking a deep breath of the fresh air, he reached down and patted Pike's neck.

"We're home, old boy. We're home."

When the sun dipped in the west, Frank didn't see or hear the Comanche warriors coming at him from behind. In one fell swoop the braves were upon him, dragging him from Pike's back and down to the dry creek bottom, where they beheaded him and left his body for the vultures. On a routine outing, the rangers found Frank and buried him near the dry stream.

Soon, the rangers' enlistments dwindled; Fort Milam went downhill and faded into memory, just like Frank Taylor and his horse, Pike. Only a stone monument four miles southwest of Marlin Falls, and the bluish light, floating near the creek bed where Frank was killed, remains, and on occasion when someone is curious enough to stop, Frank appears without his head.

From Marlin, take FM 712 (FM is the abbreviation for Farm to Market Road) about four miles southwest to FM 2027, then go south two miles to the local road. Take that road east 0.7 mile to Brazos River Falls. On the marker for Fort Milam the inscription reads: "Built at the capital of Robertson's Colony named in 1834 Sarahville De Viesca in honor of his mother, Sarah Robertson, and the Governor of Texas, Agustín Viesca. Soon after its name was changed to Milam, December 27, 1835, a Ranger company built the fort as a protection to the settlers against hostile Indians."

FORT MILAM/FORT BURLESON

In the winter of 1838, during the Christmas season, a group of families who had settled a few miles east of the old vacant Fort Milam stockade gathered to celebrate the holidays. A Comanche war party interrupted the celebration and massacred everyone in the barn: men, women, and children.

Songs of joy and peace might still be heard around midnight along the east bank of the Brazos River in Falls County, along with harsh war cries and sobs of pain that echo through the night skies.

Several weeks before the celebration, the settlers had spread the word about the huge barn dance and feast at Doris and Jim Bob Prine's homestead. Doris had baked for days to have enough pies and breads to feed the families who had promised to show up. She and her two children, Sarah and Little Jimmy, popped corn and strung it along with the berries they had picked the week before to decorate the tree Jim Bob had cut.

The day of the party, guests started arriving by noon. Jim Bob took the men out to the barn, where they started sampling the corn whiskey and tuning up the musical instruments. Tables were set up for the food the ladies brought in large baskets. Altogether, about thirty-five people showed up, counting the children.

Jim Bob played the banjo, and Lewis played the fiddle. While one neighbor played the spoons and another the jug, music filled the barn. After the music started, the men and women began dancing and the young people found partners of their own, especially one couple who had been seeing each other without their parents' permission.

Donna and Roy danced several rounds and then decided to go for a walk before they ate supper.

"I don't think we should go out there in the dark, Roy. There might be Indians out tonight. See how full the moon is? What if my pa or your pa comes out here and finds us? They won't neither one of them like it."

"Don't worry, Donna. I saw them squared off with a checkerboard in front of them. I think Mr. Prine talked them into settling their differences with a game instead of at each other's throats. He is the one who told me it'd be all right for us to take a walk. He knows how things are with us."

Donna pulled her cloak tighter around her neck and put the hood over her head as they stepped deeper into the surrounding brush.

"Aren't you cold, Roy?"

Roy rubbed his arms briskly. "Well, maybe a bit. Smells like there might be some snow in the air. Come on over here. There's a wagon pretty close to the barn and we can sit in it for a while."

Donna could feel her fingers grow numb as they walked through the crackling shrubbery. An owl hooted mournfully and a lonely nightingale took up the call. She'd heard that the Indians used birdcalls to communicate with each other, and that thought made her shiver more than the frosty air.

"Okay, let's find the wagon." She peered out into the darkness. Roy led her to the wagon, gently took her by the waist, and helped her up into the back of it.

"What are you so nervous about? Isn't this better? This way the wind won't be hitting us."

"Yes," she answered, snuggling closer. "This is better. I like it, don't you?"

"Yep, I sure do." Roy inhaled deeply.

"What are you doing?"

"You smell so pretty, Donna. I can't help myself."

Donna giggled and burrowed her head closer to his shoulder.

After sitting in the wagon for some time, Donna heard her name being called from inside the barn.

"I've got to get back in there. My mama is looking for me, and if she finds me out here, she will skin my hide."

"All right." Roy gave in and led her back inside.

Donna's mother stood in the doorway, her hands on her hips, waiting. "Where have you been, young lady? I have been hunting everywhere for you."

Smiling dreamily, Donna answered, "I've been outside getting a breath of fresh air."

Her mother looked at her scornfully. "Fresh air, my foot. You've been out there with Roy. Well, young lady, you get behind the table and set out the food we brought. The ladies have everything nearly ready to eat."

The dancing and music stopped, and Jim Bob stood on a bale of hay. "I'll offer a prayer for this fine meal when all of you gather around." He waited a few seconds and then bowed his head. "For this gathering, Lord, we give thee thanks. For this food we give thanks."

Chaos broke loose when the double doors burst open and fifty or more Comanche warriors rode through the barn, slashing with spears and knives. Donna watched in horror as they shot arrows into the bodies of the men, women, and children. Then, coming face-to-face with one of the Indians, Donna screamed. The warrior, startled for a moment, yelled back at her before he drove an arrow through her heart.

After everyone was dead, the Comanches set fire to the barn and wagons and took the horses and livestock with them.

When word of the grisly attack on the homestead reached Capt. James Daniels, he immediately made plans to build a fort on the east bank of the Brazos River.

Fort Milam, later renamed Fort Burleson, became a reality in early 1839. It was built near the home of John Marlin, east of the old Fort Milam, of cedar posts sunk into the ground in rows of two with bastions on each corner.

Capt. Joseph Daniels's Milam Guards from Houston were originally posted to the fort before Lt. William Evans and his volunteers, referred to as Travis Spies, arrived that spring. A month later, on May 6, he was joined by Capt. John Bird, who raised an additional company of men that stayed at the fort until the end of summer.

When the two companies of men were discharged, regulars from the First Infantry garrisoned Fort Milam/Fort Burleson. Lt. Col. William S. Fisher ordered the name of the fort changed on August 26, 1839, in honor of Edward Burleson, commander of the Army of the Republic of Texas.

In the following spring of 1840, Company D of the regulars with Capt. George T. Howard garrisoned the fort, and then it was later commanded by Capt. John Holliday.

In late spring of 1840, the army moved the troops to Camp Chambers and abandoned Fort Milam/Fort Burleson. The post passed from one commander to another for a couple of years until it finally fell into private hands and local citizens took control of the area.

The second fort is located two miles east and two miles south of the old Fort Milam near Marlin, Texas, in Falls County. To find it, from Marlin, Texas, take FM 712 about two miles southwest to Brazos River Falls.

FORT SHERMAN

Local citizens say that the cries of a Cherokee woman's death chant can be heard on the winds at the old Fort Sherman site. The woman, Little Creek, was killed while trying to steal meat for her hungry children.

Capt. W. B. Stout brought troops to the Cherokee Trail site in 1838 to protect the settlers against Indian depredations. Trouble between the settlers and the Cherokee and other tribes kept the whole vicinity up in arms for several years. Built on the Cherokee Crossing of Cypress Creek, Fort Sherman was little used after the

Cherokee tribe was forced out of East Texas. Many folks were buried in the cemetery that remains a part of the countryside.

After the encroachment of white settlers in the buffalo valley began driving the great shaggy beasts westward, the Cherokees and other tribes launched a bloody attack on several of the valley families. Little Creek's husband had to join this raid. He suffered wounds in the chest from the white man's bullets and died.

Little Creek sang the death song for her man, who had given her three strong sons. Her husband was the last in his family line except for his sons. That left Little Creek to provide for herself and her children. None of the boys were old enough to hunt, so she had to be both mother and father to them or marry again right away. She could not bring herself to marry yet.

On the morning after the harvest moon, she made a decision to hunt for her family. The sun had not completely opened its eyes when Little Creek slipped out of camp, carrying her bow and arrows. She wore a deerskin robe to ward off the winter winds that threatened to bring a blizzard to the Cherokee hunting grounds.

She had no success after hunting all day and was on her way back to the winter camp when she sighted Fort Sherman. The aroma of buffalo meat roasting somewhere inside the fortress coaxed Little Creek to the perimeter of the compound, where she waited until it was dark.

She reasoned that if the soldiers were cooking buffalo meat, they must have more stored away. She might be able to steal some for herself and her children. Little Creek sat huddled against the winds until darkness came upon the earth and the sun slept. When she felt she could gain entry to Fort Sherman without being noticed, she slipped into the compound and rummaged through several buildings until she found the buffalo meat she sought.

Taking only what she could readily carry, Little Creek started toward her home. The meat was heavy and she moved slowly. It was slow enough that she was noticed.

"Halt!" A soldier lifted his rifle to his shoulder. Little Creek broke into a run.

"Stop or I'll shoot!" The trooper pulled the trigger, and the report of his rifle echoed off the night sky. The bullet found its target, and Little Creek fell to her knees, but only for a moment. She stumbled through the night to her home, where she put the meat on the shelf she had made from rocks and branches. She kissed each of her children and weakly made her way to her husband's resting place, where she collapsed. Dragging herself to a sitting position, she leaned against the base of her husband's death scaffold and began chanting her own death song between coughs full of blood. A short time later Little Creek died, leaving the care of her children to the members of her family.

Now Little Creek's death chant can sometimes be heard on long winter's nights when the harvest moon is full. She mourns for the children she had to leave behind and for the loss of all that was dear to the lives of the Cherokee Nation, who were forced from their homelands.

Fort Sherman existed for only a few months. It was abandoned in 1839 after the Cherokees were forced out of East Texas. The only thing remaining of the fort by 1967 was a large, abandoned cemetery.

Fort Sherman's site is one mile north of the Cherokee Crossing of Cypress Creek and thirteen miles southwest of present-day Mount Pleasant in Titus County. To visit Mount Pleasant off Interstate 30, at the junction of US Highway 271 and State Highway 49 in East Texas, you will find the Bob Sandlin State Park and Fort Sherman Cemetery. The cemetery is located in the southwestern part of Titus County on the property of Bob Sandlin State Park. There is a chain-link fence surrounding the cemetery, and the state maintains the grounds. This cemetery is in very good condition. It is supposed to be one of the oldest cemeteries, if not the oldest, in the county. The earliest settlements in this region were in the 1830s. Fort Sherman was established nearby in 1839, and this is where the cemetery gets its name.

LITTLE RIVER FORT

Cold winter winds bring out a man of ice who melts into the memories of those who see him during the full moon near the site of the old Little River Fort.

The fort was established in November 1836. Sergeant George B. Erath and a regiment of Texas Rangers garrisoned there.

The fort covered only about a half-acre, with six or seven cabins standing against the north wall of a nine-foot-tall stockade and a square blockhouse above that for added defense. Little River Fort, like most other Texas frontier forts, was built to provide protection. Because of the location of the fort and the small number of men stationed there, it was of little help except to those in the immediate vicinity. No more than twenty men were ever stationed at the fort to help guard the settlers.

Two major skirmishes fought at the fort occurred in the first few months of 1837. In the first skirmish, a young ranger lost his life to the elements rather than to the Indians' weapons.

Ranger Curtis Green, an expert marksman, fought with fervor unmatched by the other men who battled alongside him. Curtis missed few shots, but a Comanche's well-aimed arrow broke a bone in the ranger's upper arm, making it impossible for him to hold his rifle to his shoulder.

Curtis was sent to the infirmary to be treated for his wound, but he didn't remain long. Already, falling snow blanketed the ground. Curtis felt the Indians would probably leave because of the weather, and he wanted to do his part.

"I'm a better fighter with my fists anyway," he told the man in the bed next to him.

"Curtis, you can't go out there with that arm. You'll get killed for sure."

"But what if I can get behind them and get off a couple of rounds? The Indians will think they're in crossfire, and that should buy us some time. I could slip out on old Wimpy and they'd never see me. One man on a horse isn't as big a target as two or three."

"You're crazy."

"You keep the surgeon busy. I'll slip out of here and be back before you know it."

Curtis waited until no one was looking, then he bolted out the door. He made his way to the corral at the end of the compound and squeezed through the pickets to get to his horse. Grabbing the saddle horn, he jumped up on the animal's back. The pain nearly undid him, but he rode to the far gate where only a couple of the men were holding off the savage attackers.

Needing to help at another post, the two men noticed Curtis and called to him. "Hey, Curtis, what happened to you?"

"Aw, it's nothing."

"Watch that gate. If any of them savage devils try to come in, shoot them."

"Sure, I can do that for you."

Curtis had only watched the gate for a few minutes when he saw a wagonload of settlers coming toward the fort. Opening the gate, he rode out of the stockade at a full gallop, and using his rifle like a club, he made himself a decoy by riding among the Comanches. His diversion gave the settlers a chance to escape into the fort.

He knocked several of the braves from their horses into the wet snow. The men inside the fort stopped firing to keep from hitting him with a stray bullet. Thinking the white man was crazy, the Indians retreated, leaving the battle for another day.

In the aftermath, Curtis slumped in the saddle, clutching the horn. The snow fell about his shoulders, soaking him to the skin. The rangers inside the fort rushed out and helped him dismount, then carried him to the infirmary.

A week later Curtis died of pneumonia. A burial detail carried him to the cemetery behind the Little River Fort, where he was laid to rest. Several weeks later, in April, the Comanches attacked again. The deaths on both sides were fewer than twenty.

In June 1837 the troops from Little River Fort were divided and transferred to Fort Colorado and Fort Milam to add to their defenses, leaving the farming community to make a decision: stay unprotected or leave the area. The settlers left as well.

On January 13, 1840, the War Department sent troops back to Little River Fort but failed to supply the troops properly. This failure, coupled with harsh winter weather, forced abandonment again. On July 1 the troops regrouped and returned to the fort and stayed until the following March of 1841. Total abandonment came five years later, in 1845, after only sporadic armament of Little River Fort.

In the winter of 1846, when snow was deep around it, rangers took shelter in the fort for the final time. Moses Green, owner of the land, eventually dismantled the fort completely, leaving only the ranger's spirit to occupy the legends of Little River Fort for all time.

Little River Fort was located at the junction of the Leon River and the Lampasas River in what is now Bell County. There is a historical marker at the former site of Little River Fort near Belton, Texas, in Bell County, along the east side of Interstate 35 Frontage Road.

FORT LYDAY

If you visit Fort Lyday at the rise of the full moon in the winter months, you just might see the ghost of a lone Apache brave driving several head of cattle up the banks of the North Sulphur River. Each animal in the herd slips over the edge and disappears into the deepening darkness, followed by the Indian. The warrior still seeks to take the stolen cattle to his people.

Fort Lyday was established in 1836 by Isaac Lyday to help defend the settlers and keep their stock safe from marauding Indians. The small half-acre site was comprised of several ten- by twelve-foot storerooms against one wall and similar-size cabins for living quarters scattered around the other three walls. The stockade had a community well in the middle of the grounds, and the stock pens were outside the picket palisades.

For a time in 1838 the Red River County Rangers were garrisoned at Fort Lyday to protect the fourteen families living nearby. The commanding officer of the rangers was Capt. William B. Stout. He was under orders from Gen. John H. Dryer, who commanded the Fourth Militia Brigade. The rangers under Stout made repairs to the dilapidated fort.

When threats of Indian attacks began, settlers from Cypress Creek often came to the stockade, bringing their milk cows and plow horses with them. However dangerous the Apaches tended to be, they only wanted the horses and cattle to feed their own families.

One of the settlers had brought with him several head of cattle he didn't want lost to the savages and penned them inside the stockade corrals. That same night the Apaches sent their best warrior to bring the cattle to their encampment. After making his way to the fort, the warrior left his horse in a stand of trees and crawled on his belly to the stockade. He scaled the fence and quietly made his way to the corrals. Once in the pens, he herded the cattle toward the gate he'd opened earlier. The cattle milled about, then started out of the fences. The warrior stalked along the wall to the gate and pushed the cattle through slowly. Running in the shadows, he jumped on his horse and herded the stock across the shallow water and up the bank of the North Sulphur River.

A soldier on watch had been sleeping on duty and awakened just as the brave started up the bank of the river with the cattle. He saw what was happening and sounded the alarm.

The rangers in the fort rode out in pursuit of the cattle. The soldier who spotted the Indian was a fine marksman. He stuffed the ball and wadding into the end of the rifle barrel behind the black powder and aimed at the Apache's back. As he squeezed the trigger gently, his bullet hit its mark, and the warrior fell from his horse as it reached the top of the riverbank.

The Apache's body was left for the wildlife, and after a couple of hours of searching in the darkness, the soldiers herded the cattle back to the stockade, except for three cows, which could not be found. No other attempts were made by the Indians to steal cattle from Fort Lyday.

Troops at Fort Lyday were no longer needed to protect the families, and the army abandoned it in 1843. The threat of Apache Indian attack was virtually zero in the area during the next few years.

Fort Lyday fell into decay and has not been reconstructed. Now overtaken by brush, nothing is left of the stockade and corrals to show for its service to the settlers.

When the moon begins to rise it appears to be a large orange ball in the sky. A silhouette passes across the face of the moon. Dark figures move up the riverbank to the top of the dam. Following close behind is a lone rider, dressed in buckskins. Shots ring out in the night air and a shaft of light rises to the top of the embankment. Several people in the area tell of seeing the lone Apache and how he was shot. There is a historical marker along the road near the long-gone Fort Lyday that reads:

> *Early Texas Pioneer Isaac Lyday built a fort in this area soon after settling here in 1836. The compound, located 75 mi. E and .5 mi. N. of the old Lyday crossing on the North Sulphur River, consisted of living quarters, storerooms, and a large community well. Many local families gathered inside the Fort during Indian raids. Due to an increase in these raids, the area was almost abandoned by Anglo settlers until Texas Ranger Captain William B. Stout arrived in 1838 to organize a Ranger force. Lyday was elected captain of the Company and served until 1839. Fort Lyday continued to shelter settlers until the raids subsided ca. 1843, and the fort was eventually abandoned.*

To reach the Fort Lyday marker, from Ladonia, take FM 64 east four miles to FM 904, then go north on FM 904 for four miles to a right-of-way. The site is located just east and north of Lyday's Crossing on the North Sulphur River in what is now the southwestern corner of Lamar County.

PART III

FORTS ESTABLISHED BETWEEN 1846 AND 1865

FORT MARCY

While walking along the beach near the old Fort Marcy site, don't be frightened if you come across a group of soldiers marching in the spray of the ocean waves. They are harmlessly looking for their regiment. Reports of the ancient beachcombers are spread up and down the Gulf Coast, and the stories of their existence vary. These troops' service to the army was cut short when they started across the channel from St. Joseph's Island, off the coast of Texas, with Commander Zachary Taylor.

The first burials in the Bay View Cemetery were for the eight soldiers killed en route from St. Joseph's Island, across from Corpus Christi on August 15, 1845. Zachary Taylor moved US troops, infantry, dragoons, and artillery to Corpus Christi, where he set up a camp that eventually became known as Fort Marcy. Shortly after establishing Fort Marcy, Taylor proposed abandoning the Corpus area later in February 1846. On March 11 a dense fog had covered the island while the men prepared to make the journey to set up another fort, which would be easier to defend than the fort near the lighthouse on St. Joseph's Island. Despite the bad visibility caused by the fog, Gen. Zachary Taylor ordered his men to take several boats from the island to the mainland.

Shortly after all the boats cast off, the tide became rough and two of the craft capsized; eight soldiers lost their lives. Later the same year, General Taylor received orders to move his troops to the Rio Grande, where it was thought they'd be of more use. Fort Marcy did not see any troops again until June 1849 when a partial company of dragoons was stationed at the fort.

In August 1849 a supply depot took up headquarters in the area for several months. General Persifor Smith moved the army headquarters to Fort Marcy in 1853 and abandoned it again in 1857. Southern soldiers briefly used it in 1863.

The first commander of the troops of Fort Marcy eventually became president of the United States and remains in the history books, but the troops who perished on the fateful morning crossing remain only in our memories.

A simple marker remains to bear evidence of Fort Marcy's existence. The marker is located on State Highway 136, half a mile west of the intersection with State Highway 207. Its inscription reads:

Captain R. B. Marcy commissioned in 1840 by the Federal government to establish a less hazardous route with good water on an even terrain, to be more direct from Fort Smith thru Santa Fe to the gold fields of California. This historical marker was dedicated on the path by the Rotary Club of Borger, Texas, June 19, 1956.

FORT BROWN

Originally called Fort Texas, Fort Brown was established on the Rio Grande on March 26, 1846, to help form the southern boundary of Texas. By April of the same year, soldiers had built an earthen fort with a perimeter of about eight hundred yards. It consisted of six bastions, walls more than nine feet high, and a parapet of fifteen feet.

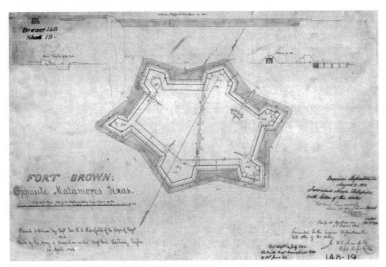

A line drawing of the Old Fort Brown

A ditch fifteen feet deep and twenty feet wide surrounded Fort Brown. Troops from the Seventh Infantry and Company I of the Second Artillery and Company E of the Third Artillery were garrisoned at the fort under the command of Maj. Jacob Brown.

When the troops led by Major Brown were intercepted by Mexican troops while taking supplies to the fort, the clash brought about the opening of the Mexican War. Major Brown was killed in a bombardment from the Mexicans on May 9, 1846. He was buried within the walls of the fortification.

In 1848, quarters for the officers and enlisted men were built, and Fort Brown became a permanent post a quarter of a mile from the earthen fort site. It boasted a brick wall called the Quarter-Master's Fence, dividing the community from the fort personnel.

Rumors of abandonment circulated in late 1848, but Indian raids continued on into 1852 and made it necessary to keep Fort Brown open. One to four companies of troops protected the settlers from Indian attacks and possible incursions into Texas by Mexico.

The early winter months of 1860 brought soon-to-be-general Robert E. Lee to Fort Brown to quell border disturbances. In March 1861 Fort Brown was temporarily abandoned by federal troops and reoccupied by troops of the state of Texas. The Civil War brought the need for rearmament of Fort Brown by Confederates in 1863.

Later in 1864, Union troops took over the fort, but one year later it was returned to the Confederacy. When the Confederate troops left for the last time, they burned most of the buildings along with the cotton bales stored in them.

After the war, in 1869, Fort Brown saw more troops move in to protect the citizens from Mexican invasion. The burned-out buildings were rebuilt of brick, including the hospital, an administration building, a large officers' quarters, and a chapel.

In 1882, Dr. William Crawford Gorgas was sent to treat the victims of one of the worst yellow fever outbreaks ever. Many settlers from the area succumbed to the dreaded disease.

Following the 1882 yellow fever epidemic, August 1906 brought another disaster. Black troops were accused of attacking the city of Brownsville. Consequences included an investigation, demand for removal of black troops, and court-martial of the troops involved. Shortly afterward the fort was transferred to the Department of the Interior by President Theodore Roosevelt, and it was converted into an experimental garden for spineless cacti.

Because of increased racial tensions, Fort Brown was later reactivated and became the headquarters for the Brownsville Military District. Guards were mobilized in 1914.

Between World Wars I and II, Fort Brown was the home of the Twelfth Cavalry. Training these men became the number one purpose for Fort Brown until 1944, when it was once more closed down.

Deactivation became official in 1945, and the fort was turned over to the army engineers. On July 7, 1946, the property of Fort Brown was released to the Federal Land Bank for farming purposes.

The Cavalry Building at Fort Brown served as a barracks until World War I.
THE LYDA HILL TEXAS COLLECTION OF PHOTOGRAPHS IN CAROL M. HIGHSMITH'S
AMERICA PROJECT, LIBRARY OF CONGRESS, PRINTS AND PHOTOGRAPHS DIVISION

On July 22, 1948, 162 acres of Fort Brown was deeded to the city of Brownsville, Texas, and it was split up accordingly. In the early 1990s the University of Texas–Pan American and Texas Southwest College were using what was left of the old fort.

While visiting Fort Brown on a quest for ghostly experiences, my friend and I were shown to the historical morgue building. It was being used as an accounting office and storage area. Workers in the building told us they'd been plagued with electrical malfunctions. As we stood talking to one woman, the lights flickered off and on at will. Electrical machinery that another lady was using quit working in the middle of a project. When the machines were checked out, no feasible explanation for the electrical failure was found.

Maybe Major Brown felt cheated at not being able to lead his men any longer and is still hanging around to battle another day. Some believe the electrical malfunctions and hauntings of the accounting office are holdovers from the yellow fever epidemic at

Fort Brown. The many dead victims of the horrible disease were laid out in the old morgue until their bodies could finally be buried.

The morgue saw much use when a group of black soldiers from the old fort allegedly attacked Brownsville on August 13, 1906. It may be that the ghostly holdovers of this incident are causing the electrical systems of the building to go haywire in protest of racial discrimination.

FORT FITZHUGH

A small log stockade built in 1847 came under the command of Texas Ranger William E. Fitzhugh to defend against marauding Indians. Fort Fitzhugh was one in a series of forts on the Texas frontier that consisted of a single row of blockhouses and a stable close by.

The site was later chosen as the county seat, to be named Liberty. However, a different site was eventually selected and named Gainesville. Many times settlers in the area rode with the rangers against attacking Indians. One such settler was a young man named Hank Johnson.

One night Hank went out with some of the other men and chased a Comanche raiding party through the countryside.

Hank had fallen from his horse, and the other men were unable to find him. They rode back to the stockade, leaving Hank, presuming him dead. A couple of days later Hank came limping into view of the fort, supporting himself with a makeshift crutch.

"Hank!" His mother ran out to meet her son. "My heavens, boy, we thought you had done got yourself killed."

"Mama, it will take more than a leg wound to get me down. Did my horse get home or did the Indians get her?"

"Smitty brought her home. She sure has been jittery since they brought her back. Can't nobody go in the barn and feed her without she starts nickering and pawing the floor. It's like she went around crying for you, and it's been the same with your old hound dog. He's done nothing except sit and howl at the stars every night since you didn't come home."

"Well, I would have been home sooner, except I had to find a limb long enough to fit me." He patted the crutch. "Would you send Jessie to get Smitty? I've got to talk to him. Still haven't figured out why they left me. I tried to tell them where I fell."

By the time Hank got the last words out, Smitty walked around the corner of the house and grabbed his chest.

"It's a ghost, Mrs. Johnson! Get out of there!"

"Naw, Smitty. It's Hank."

"Hank, is that really you?" Smitty felt Hank's arms.

"Yep, I'm home, Smitty." Hank accepted the bear hug from his boyhood friend.

"Why did you boys leave me out there?" Hank asked.

Smitty grabbed his friend by the arm and helped him into the house.

"Honest, Hank, we looked for you and then we found old Bell and your saddle was empty. What would you have thought?" Smitty looked at the fire in the fireplace. "We thought you died out there, Hank. We truly did. Where did you get off to?"

"I rolled down in a draw, and I guess the grass was tall enough it covered me up."

Several weeks later Hank felt fit enough to leave the fort. Another raiding party made off with several cows and horses, and against his mother's wishes, Hank rode out with the troops to fight the Indians and recover the livestock.

Major Fitzhugh took charge of the tracking party and tried to make sure they didn't leave anyone behind. When the raiders turned to fight, they forced the men from the fort to make another retreat. Hank disappeared again. This time he was wounded in the shoulder. Mr. Fitzhugh and his men found him trying to crawl up the bank of the creek bed.

"Hank, you'd better quit gettin' lost," Smitty said. "Someday, we might not find you again." He helped his friend into his saddle.

"Oh, don't worry about me. I'll be like my old hound dog. I'll find my way home if you and the other men don't find me right away."

According to the story, several weeks later Hank, still on the mend, decided to go fishing. Relaxation and some fresh air would do him a world of good, he reasoned with his mother.

Hank, followed by his dog, walked down to the creek. He threw out his fishing line and leaned against a tree, enjoying the brilliant sunshine. He dozed off, and a while later his dog gave a low, throaty growl. The hound alerted him, but before he could react, several Comanche braves sprang out from the brush. A hail of arrows plunged into Hank's body, and then they shot his dog. Hank managed to crawl a few feet from the water to the old dog. The hound, with an arrow sticking out of his leg, made his way home without Hank.

His mother alerted Smitty, and the men at the settlement formed a search party. The next morning they found young Hank's body. The expression of horror on his face caused the men to be hesitant about taking him back to the fort for his mother and sister to see. They buried him with his fishing pole next to the water's edge at Elm Creek.

Smitty carved a headstone and placed it at Hank's grave. In a downpour later the same year, the headstone washed away, and no one ever replaced it.

Many people have reported seeing Hank wandering through the night, carrying his fishing pole and looking for his home. Men on horseback, stopping to spread their blankets on the bank of Elm Creek, have spoken of seeing Hank in the shadowy moonlight, a gruesome look of horror on his face. Those who saw the apparition fled the area, some leaving their bedrolls behind.

Some say even dogs refuse to go near the creek bed. Hank's body may lie at the bottom of the shallow grave; however, his spirit is here, searching for his way home.

Although the fort was abandoned in 1850, the city of Gainesville continued to prosper. In 1948, the local Boy Scout unit, to mark the location where Fort Fitzhugh had once stood, donated a plaque. A well and a caved-in ammunition dump, which may have been part of the original stockade, are all that remain.

Take a trip to Gainesville, Texas, in Cooke County and about three miles southeast of the city, you will find the marker donated by the local Boy Scouts.

EL FORTIN/FORT LEATON

The legends of Fort Leaton are of a bloody nature, and the apparitions stem from violent and vicious men who carved out a livelihood from others' pain and strife.

Many believe Ben Leaton's ghost haunts the area around the fort along with the ghost of Edward Hall, Mrs. Leaton's second husband, who became the murder victim of Leaton's friend John Burgess. Mrs. Leaton is sometimes seen in her rocking chair at the kitchen window. A number of people who have visited or worked there have told of evil feelings at Fort Leaton. Violence seems to have stayed with the fort over the years.

Ben Leaton, a bounty hunter in Mexico, collected Indian scalps for the Mexican government for years before settling on the Texas side of the Rio Grande. In 1848 he married and built a massive fort to protect himself and his family from the Indians whose tribal members he'd killed and scalped. He also felt he needed protection from the Mexicans he'd worked for because he had often angered them with some of his dealings.

After his death, Ben Leaton's widow married a customs agent, Edward Hall. They lived in the same house where she and Leaton lived before he died.

Hall found himself in a monetary bind and borrowed money from Ben's old friend John Burgess. Using the fort for collateral, Hall either couldn't or wouldn't pay back the loan, and Burgess contracted to have Edward Hall murdered. Afterward, Burgess called in his loan and took over the fort.

Later, Burgess married Mrs. Leaton-Hall. After he moved into the fort with her and her son, Bill Leaton, he became agitated one night and went for a walk. While John was strolling in the compound, he stopped cold when he saw a dark, mystical figure approach from the stockade wall.

"Who is it?" he asked, the sound of his own voice sending shivers up his spine.

"That's right, John, you should be afraid. It's me, Ben Leaton. You're not seeing things. You'd better repent. I'm warning you," Leaton's ghost spoke quietly.

Fear mounted in John. "What are you talking about?" he whispered.

"You are headed for an extremely unpleasant future." The shrouded figure smiled with an evil light in its eyes and returned to the wall, where it vanished.

The next day John Burgess began building a chapel in the same room where he'd had Hall killed. A month or so later, Burgess stood in the doorway of the chapel he'd just finished. Calmness washed over him. No way could Leaton's ghost appear to him again. He was safe now. His worry would no longer keep him awake at night. He closed the door on the new sanctuary and went down the hall to the kitchen, where his wife sat rocking in her chair.

"Is it finished?" Martha continued to rock.

"It's done." John bent and kissed his wife softly on the top of the head.

"Good, perhaps we can all have some peace of mind now."

"Yes, Martha. I'm going to read for a bit. Is there coffee made?"

"I'll bring it to you, John. Go along."

John Burgess sought his own rocking chair to relax. Every day for a week after he finished the chapel, his routine didn't change. On the setting of the sun, he sat and read the Bible with a cup of coffee on the table beside him. One evening he was distracted by a noise outside his window, and when he started to see what was going on, his stepson, Bill Leaton, charged through the house firing his revolver at anything that moved.

"John Burgess, rot in hell!" were the last words Burgess heard before his wife's son shot him through the heart.

In 1926, the Burgess family abandoned the Fort Leaton compound, but the fort remains a thorn in the side of the community with its evil past. The ghost of Edward Hall has been seen in the room where the man murdered him many years before. Some say Hall returned to make Burgess build the chapel while others think it might have been Leaton himself who had come back to warn Burgess of the consequences of sin.

Visitors to the Fort Leaton compound report the rattling of chains in the stable area, like someone might be unharnessing a team of horses. This could be any of Leaton's hired help, who often endured beatings for not doing something to suit the boss.

Other stories of Fort Leaton include an accident involving a horseman caught in a sudden storm near the fort. Apparently, when he went to pull on his rain slicker, it caused his horse to spook, and the rider, thrown from his saddle, entangled his foot in the stirrup. The horse ran off, dragging the man behind. Screams of agony and terror echoed through the night. The horse, wild-eyed and terrified of the noise and its rider dangling to the ground, ran erratically through the open territory. Eventually the body of the rider was torn to shreds and dropped loose from the stirrup.

The next day when men from the nearby ranch came looking for their coworker, they found his body several hundred feet from his head, which was lying wedged between a broken tree limb and a huge boulder. The look of pain on his face made the other men cringe. They used the remnants of the slicker to carry the man's head to his body.

Now, whenever a sudden thunderstorm hits the area, some claim that the headless horseman rides the Fort Leaton grounds. His snowwhite horse gallops around the area, and the horseman's black rain slicker flaps wildly in the wind.

In the past, homeless families often took shelter in the abandoned Fort Leaton compound during thunderstorms. Once an older couple visited Fort Leaton State Park, and they told of the time they took up residence at the fort for a while.

In the early 1920s, as a newlywed couple, they came to the fort for shelter. With no job and no place to live, they decided to stay at the fort like they'd heard others had done. They told of nights

This adobe structure, which was built at Fort Leaton in the 1830s, now serves as the western-side visitor center for Big Bend Ranch State Park.
THE LYDA HILL TEXAS COLLECTION OF PHOTOGRAPHS IN CAROL M. HIGHSMITH'S AMERICA PROJECT, LIBRARY OF CONGRESS, PRINTS AND PHOTOGRAPHS DIVISION

inside the fort when they would be awakened by the sound of dishes being thrown to the floor and broken. When either checked to see what might be happening, nothing seemed to be out of place, and they were the only ones around. The couple left after a few days to find other living quarters when they became too nervous to stay where vengeful ghosts seem to still be hanging around.

Supposedly, when Ben Leaton lived in the fortress, he buried large amounts of gold, made during his bounty-hunting days, somewhere in the compound. Gold seekers from across Texas and other areas came to the old fort to search for Leaton's stash, and they dug many holes in the compound. After the Parks and Wildlife Department took over the operation of the fort, they had to fill in the holes before allowing the public inside.

One hole, in particular, had been deeply dug. It had been filled with garbage from many years of dumping by everyone who passed by. Workers had to be hired to clean out and cover the space. After only a few days of digging out and filling the gaping hole, the workers quit. They claimed it felt like they were being pulled into the pit. They never returned for their paychecks.

On one of the most scenic routes in the southeast, Fort Leaton offers many facilities at the park, including historic ruins, restored rooms, interpretive exhibits with audio-visual programs, shaded picnic tables, a five-mile interpretive trail, and restrooms. The gift shop is also located on the grounds.

The Barton Warnock Environmental Education Center serves the public as a visitor center for Fort Leaton and the Big Bend Ranch State Park. Fort Leaton is four miles southeast of Presidio on the River Road to the Big Bend on FM 170 in Presidio County. It was deeded to the state in 1967 and not opened to the public until 1978.

On June 18, 1973, the area was put on the Register of Historic Places listings in Presidio County. It is open to the public daily from 8:00 a.m. to 4:30 p.m. seven days a week year-round. It is closed on Christmas Day. Entrance fees apply.

FORT INGE

Mist rolled up from the rain-soaked ground as the overland mail coach rumbled along the route. Ever watchful for Indians, who generally attacked at the drop of a hat, the shotgun rider shaded his face from the morning sun. When the driver cracked his whip over the backs of the team of six horses pulling the coach, Dan Sharp dodged the sometimes-errant tip of the long snaky length of leather.

He'd ridden this route several times with Bob Doss, and they'd never had any trouble. This morning, though, he'd awakened with a nagging feeling in the pit of his stomach.

Jumping at every odd sound, Dan clutched his rifle, ready to fire in an instant. He had no desire to lose his scalp to some savage, especially now that he and Mary were going to be married. They both lived at Fort Inge, separately of course, and for several months they had been courting. No one would criticize Mary for marrying again. Her husband, Zeb Inge, had been killed in 1846 at Resaca de la Palma, and she was still a fine figure of a woman.

The thought of Mary made him smile. He pictured her yellow hair gleaming in the Texas sunlight, and his heart skipped a beat. Mary was the kind of woman a man wanted to take care of and spend the rest of his life with, regardless of whether she'd been married before.

Suddenly rifle shots rang out through the countryside. Bullets plugged the coach. Dan took aim at a bush alongside the road and fired. He heard a deep thud, as bullets from his own rifle hit their target. A half-dressed Comanche savage rose, then sprawled facedown in the dirt. More shots splintered the coach from behind, and Indians swarmed from every direction. Dan turned in his seat and began firing as the Comanches gained on them. Then a strange feeling came over Dan. He felt the presence of someone crawling atop the coach with him, and then heard the fire from a rifle. When he looked around no one sat beside him except Bob. He heard more shots but saw no gun and the Indians fell from their horses with each round being fired. Soon the Comanches' horses were running wild without riders, and the firing stopped.

Bob cracked his whip again, urging the team to a faster pace. "Dan, I didn't know you could shoot that good."

"I didn't."

"Well, who else could've done it? You and I are the only ones here, and I was too busy driving this team of horses trying to outrun the devils."

Dan shook his head. "It wasn't me, Bob. I only shot twice." He turned to the top of the coach again and swiped at the perspiration burning his eyes.

"Yes, Dan, it was me."

"What did you say, Bob?"

"I didn't say anything. What's the matter with you?"

Bob frowned at the man who had been his partner for nearly seven years.

"Nothing. Only the sun I guess." Dan turned to the top of the stage and looked out across the vast prairie.

A soft whisper drifted past his ear. "It was me, Dan, Zeb Inge. Take care of Mary for me, will you?"

Dan touched his ear and looked around once more. He saw a figure, shrouded in dust, standing on top of the coach. The man's uniform, with a lieutenant's insignia, was immaculate except for a small hole over his heart, where the sparkle of sunlight shone through. The apparition winked and vanished instantly.

"Get these horses moving, Bob." Dan turned quickly from the sight on top of the coach.

The remainder of the trip was uneventful, and the mail service continued to get through without trouble until Fort Inge closed in 1861. Dan and Mary married in the spring of 1850. Dan never told anyone but Mary about the dusty morning along the mail route.

Capt. Sidney Burbank of the First US Infantry opened Fort Inge on March 13, 1849, and named it after his lifelong friend, Lt. Zebulon M. P. Inge. In 1861 troops were withdrawn from the fort.

The army reoccupied Fort Inge from 1866 to February 28, 1869. At one time the Texas Rangers used it for their camp.

In 1961, Fort Inge was taken over by Uvalde County and became the Fort Inge Historical Site. The site was added to the National Register of Historic Places in 1985.

Today Uvalde County runs Fort Inge as a park. It is open only on the weekends. Visitors can explore Fort Inge's parade ground, ruins of original post buildings, and some ruins of the wall constructed around the area during the American Civil War. Other parts of the wall have been reconstructed to give a sense of where it stood. There are a few monuments and information signs on the site. Fort Inge hosts Fort Inge Days every year.

The park also features some picnic areas and hiking trails. It is located on the Leona River and lies at the base of what was once an active volcano millions of years ago. To visit Fort Inge's ruins and the park, take State Highway 140 southeast out of Uvalde and drive approximately one-and-a-quarter miles to the Fort Inge Historical Park entrance. Follow the road in for about two-tenths of a mile.

BLAIR'S FORT

On certain nights when the moon is full, echoes of laughter and singing can be heard coming from a spot where Blair's Fort once stood. A small cabin appears when the moon rises higher in the sky. The cabin erupts in flames, and cries of agony shatter the darkness. If the night is cloudless, fleeting glimpses of a man dressed in black can be seen.

Blair's Fort, built in 1860, was a family fort, built to protect the settlers and citizens who already lived in the area. For Sadie, pretty and lively, life in the small family fort was beyond her endurance. She longed to dance and sing, and she especially longed for the company of young men.

Not only was life within the walls restrictive for Sadie, the hours spent on her knees, forced into prayer by her father, were endless.

He constantly dressed in black, and his eyes glittered while he shrieked sermons of hellfire and brimstone. The adults called him the Apostle; the frightened children called him the Preacher Man.

Sadie, tiring of her drab existence, left the fort to find a new life. Sadly, her new life began only a short distance from the home she left. She found a cabin among a grove of trees and with two friends established a "place" for gentlemen to relax. The cabin was near a stage line, and Sadie and her ladies profited rather well. When news of the ladies' youth and beauty spread, settlers, cowboys, and drifters found their way to the small, accommodating house.

The reverend tried everything within his power to bring Sadie back to Blair's Fort, to turn her aside from her new life of sin. Sadie steadfastly refused. Nearly crazed with mortification, the preacher exiled himself in his cabin, leaving only when the darkness concealed his shame.

One night when he crept through the gates, away from Blair's Fort, he was followed by a young boy from the fort. His curiosity was greater than his fear of the Preacher Man. The driving interest of youth led him to the perimeter of Sadie's cabin; his young thirst for carnal knowledge held him there.

Occupants of the cabin went about their business of entertaining well into the cold December evening.

Women's tinkling laughter and men's drunken guffaws rose above the sound of a bawdy tune banged out on a piano in sore need of tuning. A lantern blazed in each window, like a beacon in the night to any weary man who passed their way.

Crouched behind bushes, the mesmerized boy peered through the darkness as he saw the Preacher Man move about to and from the cabin. The bobbing light of a lantern marked his agitated passage. At last he stood before the door and turned up his lamp. In the sudden glow, the boy saw a heaping pile of wood before the door and under the windows. With a shout, the Preacher Man threw the lantern against the door and it burst into flames. He reached into the fire, and then he flung burning branches onto the pile under each window.

Screams of horror and agony sent the boy racing back to Blair's Fort. He turned and looked over his shoulder. The cabin door fell inward, and the Preacher Man walked into the inferno.

In the early 1920s during the Desdemona oil boom in Eastland County, another house of ill repute burned to the ground under suspicious circumstances.

Working until the wee hours of the mornings, the girls in Miss Janie's house invariably slept late into the next day after a long night's work. Miss Janie herself worked, as did her stepdaughter and three other girls. Miss Janie was the widow of a preacher. When her husband passed, Miss Janie determined not to be left out of the wealth. She decided she would benefit from the oil boom like others in the area, and she opened her home to gentlemen who needed a quiet place to rest after a hard day's work.

Built near the site of the old fort, Miss Janie's house was a comfortable place to live and work, and the girls in her employ were paid well. One of her girls had two sons. Most of the time the boys slept in the barn or the apartment at the back of the house when it wasn't in use by one of the girls. Often the boys had no shoes, and their clothes were torn and crudely patched, while Miss Janie and her ladies dressed in fine gowns bought with their ill-gotten gains.

One night in mid-December, the boys were sleeping in the barn when the crowd in the house was especially large. The older of the boys, Jake, seethed with anger at their mother for putting them out in the barn with only one blanket to share.

"The customers will need the quilts and blankets," she told him.

After the last visitor left, Jake and his little brother crept from the barn and started toward the house and warmth. They stopped, frightened, at the sight of a large, dark figure stacking kindling up around the base of the house and setting fire to it.

"What do you think you are doing?" Jake demanded.

The man, dressed entirely in black from his large floppy hat to the boots on his feet, stopped in his tracks and then whirled to face the boys. The man in black stared, his eyes burning like red embers. The boys stumbled backwards, falling to the ground. He floated off into the night, vanishing from sight.

Stunned by what they'd seen, the boys lay motionless on the ground for a few moments before leaping to their feet and running to the burning house to alert the sleeping women. The women grabbed their nearest garments and began running out of the house. Their screams of terror split the December air. Shortly afterward, the women, dressed in skimpy nightgowns, huddled together for warmth while an icy rain began to fall.

Although a fire engine came, the blaze could not be extinguished before the house was a total loss. Miss Janie, having heard stories about the Preacher Man, never rebuilt her house, and the boys never saw her again.

Today, the fort is gone with no traces of the log house anywhere to be found except on certain December nights when the Preacher Man is also seen.

Blair's Fort was located on South State Highway 16 near present-day Desdemona in Eastland County. No markers were ever set showing where the fort was sited; however, the old-timers can probably show you where to look and more than one might tell you about the Preacher Man and Sadie's house.

FORT TERRETT

When the sun is high in the noon sky, picnickers have witnessed another long-ago couple spreading their blanket on the grassy pasture and having their own picnic until suddenly they pick up their belongings and run into the bright afternoon air. They are seen only on sunny summer days.

The shortest-lived fort in Texas's history was Fort Terrett, also known as Camp Terrett. It had been built too far off the beaten path to be of any strategic help to the settlers needing protection from marauding Indians. Nonetheless, in early February 1852, troops manned the fort with the intent to protect the citizens between Fort Clark and Fort McKavett. For a brief few months in 1852, soldiers and their families living at Fort Terrett often had picnics.

Lt. Jackson Harris and Marny Ford had married in secrecy a couple of days before he was to go out into the field with his regiment. After courting for several months, neither of them wanted to wait, but Marny's parents were not happy about their only child marrying an army man. Like two children, they left the safety of the fort to enjoy the springlike weather, giggling and laughing and taking a picnic lunch with them. They had barely finished their meal when they were caught in the midst of a raiding Comanche war party.

Racing to the buggy, Lieutenant Harris practically tossed Marny into the buggy, and then he sprang onto the seat and whipped the horses into a full gallop toward the gates of Fort Terrett. Marny clung tightly to Harris's arm and cried out, frightened for their lives as he urged the horses to a faster pace. A hail of bullets and arrows fell around them.

Only moments from the safety of the compound, an arrow plunged into Harris's chest. He slumped in the seat against Marny.

She grabbed the reins, prying them from his fingers, and slapped the horses with the reins, urging them to run faster. The gates of Fort Terrett swung open and Marny drove the horses inside, barely ahead of the savages.

During the melee, Marny's pleas for help went unnoticed by the soldiers defending the fort. Pressing her lace handkerchief against the flow of blood from Jackson's chest, she waited for the post doctor.

"You'll be all right, Jackson. I will have it no other way." Marny tried to smile.

"I know, Marny, I . . ."

Before he could answer, several men came and quickly whisked him away to the hospital. Marny's handkerchief fluttered to the ground to be trodden under the feet of the troopers. Following her husband to the hospital, Marny waited outside the tent as Jackson died.

The military troops abandoned Fort Terrett in late February 1854.

Many years later a young couple on a picnic at the fort found part of a bloodstained silk lace handkerchief with initials on the corner.

Jason picked up the piece of cloth. "Hey, look, Macy, is this yours? See here are your initials. I didn't know you'd been out here before."

"That's not mine." Macy took the scrap of fabric and examined it closely.

"I wonder whose blood is on this?" Macy folded the cloth and tucked it into her pocket.

"Beats me. Let's eat."

Jason carried the basket of food while Macy spread the blanket on the grassy spot they'd chosen. Jason fished a drumstick out of the basket and ate it while Macy prepared the rest of the picnic lunch. Jason grinned at her, surprised.

"Gosh, Macy. I didn't know you could cook this good." He popped the top on their soft drinks and bit into another drumstick.

He frowned at her as she concentrated on the fabric she'd pulled from her pocket.

"What gives, Macy?"

"What? Oh, sorry." She stuffed the material back into her pocket and focused on Jason. "Nothing to cooking, really. I went to the local grocery store and bought it already cooked." Macy winked at him and laughed. Her laughter seemed to bounce off the low-hanging afternoon clouds and linger on the breeze.

"What was that?"

"Better yet, who was that?"

Jason and Macy looked at each other and then toward a stand of brush where the laughter still seemed to echo. Drawn to it, Macy stood and walked slowly toward the sound. She took in the strange sight of a young couple in antique clothing sitting on the ground. Even stranger, was the horse and buggy waiting nearby. Coming up beside her, Jason whispered, "Who is that? And why are they dressed so funny?"

Macy shrugged. "I don't know. Lots of people come here to have a picnic. Or, it could be one of those reenactment games." She turned to leave when the young couple she had been watching sprang to their feet and dashed to the buggy.

As the young man lifted the girl into the vehicle, she and Macy locked gazes.

"Macy, that's you!" Jason cried, causing Macy to look away.

Macy felt in her pocket for the strip of silk with the initials on it and smiled. Now she knew to whom the handkerchief had belonged.

"No, Jason. It had to be my great-grandmother Ford, before she married."

"What are you talking about? Your great-grandmother, my foot. That woman looked just like you."

Macy related the story of her great-grandmother Marny Ford and Lieutenant Harris.

"It's a story of love that's been passed down from my great-grandmother to my grandmother and then to my mother and me. Perhaps she wanted us to find the handkerchief. It had to be my great-grandmother's way of telling me the story is true. Some of the people in our family say that Miss Marny had loved Lieutenant Harris until the day she died, and my grandfather was a product of their love for each other. After all, he was a Ford and she married a Laird. You see, Lieutenant Harris died of his wounds that night."

"Well, how could that be?"

"I have been told that my great-grandmother and the lieutenant had only been married a day or two when he got killed. I'll bet you my grandfather was already on the way and they didn't even know it."

"You mean your grandfather was Lieutenant Harris's son and not your . . ."

"Well, they were human and they were married, if for only a short time."

"I wonder how things really were back in the eighteen hundreds. Do you think you might like to go to one of those reenactments they have sometimes?"

She smiled at him. "Sure, why not, but right now it looks like it's about to rain."

Terrett is a privately owned area where the owner still uses some of the stone buildings from the fort. The site where Fort Terrett stood is located approximately thirty miles from Sonora, Texas, in Sutton County about two miles north of Interstate 10. Since it is privately owned, you need permission to enter there.

FORT DUNCAN

At the intersection of Garrison and Adams Streets in the city of Eagle Pass, a tall willowy figure sometimes can be seen searching for her children, calling their names and weeping. She intently studies the children who pass. If anyone approaches her, she dissolves and stays away for several months until she begins her search again for the children whose lives she took when she feared the Indians.

Like most of the West Texas frontier forts, Fort Duncan had to be established to protect the settlers from the Indians and bandits in the area. It set up a line of defense on March 27, 1849. Federal troops garrisoned at Fort Duncan until March 20, 1861, when it closed during the Civil War. Again in 1868 troops were sent to man the fort.

Jim Franks and his wife, Gwendolyn, chose to live in their own cabin outside the compound of Fort Duncan rather than within the relative safety of the walls.

Gwendolyn would have it no other way, and she and the children would stay at the cabin while he rode out on patrol. No matter how much he insisted she go to the fort, she would stay at home. Any doubts Jim Franks might have had faded at Gwendolyn's insistence. Being an army wife, she showed much strength.

Years of being an army family had taught both of them much. When he told her they were moving to Texas to help establish a new fort, she immediately wanted to know the details. How long did he think it would be before he'd send for her? Were they going to have a home outside the post?

She had adjusted with each new post, until they came to Fort Duncan. She kept her anxieties to herself, not wanting him to worry about her and the children.

Jim rode out on patrol, and Gwendolyn watched until he reached the inside of the fort gates, where he would join other troops. An uneasy feeling settled across her shoulders like a heavy mantle; pausing for a moment to think about it, she shrugged it off and went about her work. She hated the thought of his being gone on patrol constantly, although the other soldiers who protected Fort Duncan weren't far away. Besides, she did know how to hitch the team to the wagon. With the Apache on the prowl though, it might not be safe trying to get to the fort if any trouble came up.

Jim would be back in a couple of hours, and they would have some time before he had to ride out again. Night patrol made her more anxious, and her fear grew each time he left.

The evening before she had heard a raccoon in back of the house and nearly panicked. She scrubbed the clothes harder, needing to get her mind off the coming nightfall. Jim returned with supplies, helped her store them in the root cellar, and played with the baby a moment before he had to ride out again.

"I'll be gone until late tomorrow morning. Depends on how far the colonel wants to ride out." Jim kissed his children, then Gwendolyn.

"Take care of your mommy, Amy."

The small girl nodded and smiled brightly.

The night would be long, and Gwendolyn would keep the vigil like every other time he left her alone at night. She finished the day's work before the sun dipped below the horizon. It always seemed to fade more quickly after Jim left on his patrol.

Gwendolyn called the children in after feeding the cow and locking the chickens in the coop. Maybe the raccoon wouldn't visit tonight.

No wind made for a rare day in West Texas, and this night was absolutely still. Studying the setting sun, Gwendolyn noticed an unusual silence at the time of day when most birds were singing.

Drowning in the horizon, the sun slipped past the mesquite brush and Gwendolyn shivered, closing the tiny windows of the cabin to keep out the darkness of night and the even darker fear.

She fed the children and cleaned up after the meal before undressing them and putting them to bed. Later, she sat in the rocker with her lap full of yarn and needles. Occasionally she stopped knitting on Amy's sweater to listen for the chirp of crickets. No sounds could be heard. Puzzled by the continuing silence, she tried to stay alert.

She didn't like the frightening quiet. Fear gripped her heart, twisting it like an iron fist. She moved to the window and cracked the shutter slightly, peering out into the darkness. A slight movement beside the barn startled her. She froze. Could it be? She strained to see. No, she shook her head; it was only her imagination. Nothing moved out there except maybe a pesky raccoon. She sat back in her rocker and knitted while the moon rose higher, seeping pale light into the cabin through the cracks in the shutters and around the doors. Jim would have to fix those before winter.

Waiting for daylight to come, Gwendolyn suffered while the night grew longer. Every noise from outside intensified in her mind, and each time she climbed out of her chair to see what made the noise, she saw nothing.

She tried to figure out what made her jumpy. Taking the rifle from the wall over the fireplace, she checked it. Loaded, she breathed a sigh of relief. Maybe, though, she should have the children sleep in the main room, where she could keep an eye on them. She'd heard stories of Indians sneaking into a house to steal the children and make slaves out of them or raise them to be savages. They wouldn't take her babies.

Lifting the baby from the crib, she woke Amy and Garvin. Amy stumbled into the front room of the cabin, rubbing her eyes, looking up at her mother trustingly. Gwendolyn rocked baby Jim while Amy and Garvin slept on a pallet at her feet. Shadows from the fire in the fireplace danced on the wall. Exhaustion from the day's chores and her worry overtook her. She dozed lightly.

Jerking awake, she frightened the baby and he began to cry. Gwendolyn covered his mouth with her hand and whispered to the child, "Hush, sweet one. Don't cry." Soon the baby grew limp in her arms and his crying stopped. Awakened by the baby's cries, Amy sat up on the pallet and glanced around. She studied her mother's ashen face, and seeing the wild look in her eyes, Amy began to whimper.

"What's wrong, mama?"

"The Indians are out there. Now be quiet and don't say anything." Frightened of the Indians, the child lay back on the pallet, listening to her mother singing to the baby before drifting off to sleep again.

Sometime in the night Gwendolyn put baby Jim on the pallet with the other two children. Amy stirred and whimpered in her sleep. To keep the child quiet, Gwendolyn took a knife and cut Amy's throat. Garvin coughed, and his fate became sealed the same as his sister's had been.

The one thing that would tell the Indians they were alone, Gwendolyn thought, would be noise. They must be strong. They had to stay quiet.

The morning dawned clear and bright. Gwendolyn sat with the rifle across her lap, ready to use it at the slightest provocation. Hearing the familiar hoof beats of Jim's horse, she flew out of the rocking chair and through the door into his arms. Relieved he had come home early, she kissed him.

Jim searched for a glimpse of the children, who were usually playing in the yard. "Where are the children, Gwendolyn?"

"The Indians were here last night, Jim. The children wouldn't keep quiet. I put them to bed in front of the fireplace on a pallet. The Indians finally went away. The children haven't awakened yet. I let them sleep late this morning since it was a long night."

The trembling in her voice and the distant look in her eyes alerted Jim to trouble. Concerned for his children, he hurried into the house to find the three children dead on their pallet. Their blood had soaked through the quilt to stain the wooden floor.

Grief-stricken, he sat down hard on the fireplace hearth. Only then did Gwendolyn realize what she had done. She staggered and slipped into her rocking chair, refusing to move until she died three months later.

Gwendolyn's ghost has been seen many times since, carrying the baby wrapped in a blanket, calling for Amy and Garvin in the Eagle Pass area. She walks on the wind, while it blows across the Fort Duncan marker, with a look of horror on her face. Some call her La Llorna because she roams the area searching for her children.

In 1933, the fort closed and the US government still owned the land. The city of Eagle Pass was allowed to develop and maintain the old post as a public park. The federal government allowed this with the condition that it could reclaim the post for military or other reasons at any time. However, two years later, the government gave the property to the city.

Fort Duncan in now a state park, and the site was listed in the National Register of Historic Places in 1971. The site contains a dozen buildings, including a stone magazine, stone stables, and adobe officers' quarters. The old headquarters building now serves as a museum. Fort Duncan Museum is now open at 310 Bliss Drive in Eagle Pass, Texas. The hours of operation are Tuesday through Saturday from 11:00 a.m. to 5:00 p.m.

FORT DAVIS

The unexpected scent of roses filled a downtown gift shop.

"Alice is back," one of the clerks, Jane Fletcher, proclaimed, smiling faintly at her coworkers.

The new clerk looked toward the door. "Where? I didn't see anyone come in."

"No, but Alice is here. Can't you smell the roses?"

Faith Best nodded. "Well, as a matter of fact, I do smell them." She lowered her voice. "I thought you had on some of the rose perfume they sell at the corner drugstore or something."

"No," Jane said. "It's Alice Walpole. She comes in here every once in a while. I think she knows when I've had word from my parents in Alabama."

"Jane, I think you've slipped a cog or something. For goodness' sake, who are you talking about?"

"Well, if you had studied the brochure about Fort Davis and had bothered to ask more questions, you'd know about the old fort and Alice Walpole."

"Well, I didn't ask before, but I'm asking now. Tell me what you're talking about, would you please?"

Jane took a deep breath and started telling Faith the story. "Alice Walpole was a young bride who followed her husband from her home in Alabama to far West Texas when he was sent to Fort Davis. This was an especially desolate area of Texas where Indians as well as Mexican raiders from across the border ran rampant. It was no place for a genteel lady like Alice.

"Alice lived on the Fort Davis grounds with her husband in a small house down on Officers' Row. Hers was a lonely, hard life. Oftentimes she had only the other officers' wives for company while her husband spent most of his time on patrol, searching for marauding Indians or Mexican bandits."

For once, Faith listened instead of talking.

"One particularly lonely day in early April 1861, after an especially harsh winter, Alice found the longing for her Alabama home unbearable. She missed the beautiful flowers she figured must be blooming in the balmy warmth of her mother's garden. Nothing but cactus and yuccas were able to grow in the harsh dry ground surrounding the area near Fort Davis.

"While out for a walk, Alice thought she caught the faint scent of roses wafting down from the surrounding mountains. She remembered cutting the roses from her mother's garden to bring inside for the hall table and the dinner table as well. White roses were her favorite, and her mother's roses were beautiful.

"Determined to have roses in her own home, Alice struck out toward the mountains, her blue woolen cloak wrapped around her shoulders. She followed the scent filling the air. Crossing the barren desert land, she climbed into the mountainous region over jagged rocks and ravines. She walked for hours, reasoning that the Indians were probably far away, running from her husband's patrol. Alice disappeared, and was never seen again. Nobody knows if she died from exposure or if the Mexicans or Indians took her life. No doubt she never found the roses here in the mountains around Fort Davis.

"When her husband's patrol returned the same evening and he found her gone, he searched the fort for her. Not finding her, he reported her disappearance to the commanding officer. A rescue party began a weeklong search for Alice, but it proved fruitless. They found her blue cloak about halfway toward the mountains.

"Several months later, Alice was seen one afternoon, strolling past the officers' quarters in her long woolen cloak carrying a bouquet of roses. The air smelled strongly of the heavy scent of roses as she passed. The soldier on duty noticed her slipping past his post, and when he tried to stop her, she disappeared without a trace. Thinking something seemed familiar about her, the guard recognized her from a dance at the post from the year before.

"The same day, Union soldiers fired upon Fort Sumpter, and word reached the commander of Fort Davis. He received resignation letters from seven of his officers, including Lieutenant Walpole. They were going east to fight for the Confederacy.

"During the confusion in his office, receiving word of the war starting, and nearly every one of his officers resigning, someone slipped into his office and left a vase with seven white roses in it. Seven white roses, for seven Confederates going off to war.

"No one knew how the roses came to be placed on his desk, but they figured Alice's ghost left them.

"Many times afterward, the fragrance of roses was noticed at some of the young women's sewing circles or when the wives of Fort Davis gathered to reminisce about their homes in the South with their lovely gardens. They would smell the fragrance, and they knew Alice had come to visit. Alice has also been known to have appeared at the homes of lonely or homesick young wives before Fort Davis closed permanently in 1867.

"Now whenever white roses are spotted at an unexpected time of year or if the scent of roses is particularly strong on the breeze anywhere near Fort Davis, it is believed Alice Walpole's ghost is out visiting again.

"Perhaps Alice found her beloved white roses when she became lost forever in the mountains around Fort Davis."

Faith sighed at the beautiful story and wiped away a stray tear. "I never heard anything so sad in my life, Jane. Next time I see a rose bush, I'll be sure to think of Alice."

Officers' Row at Fort Davis

Troops from this fort helped to open up the area to settlement and they protected the folks along the San Antonio to El Paso road.

Fort Davis served as a military post from 1854 until 1891, when the troops rode out for the final time, and is one of the best-preserved historic fort sites in the Southwest. The fort is twenty-one miles from Marfa to the south on US Highway 90 or State Highways 17 and 118.

If you are traveling from the north, take Interstate 10 to the historic site. From the west, you can get to Fort Davis on State Highways 505, 166, and 17.

CAMP COLORADO

At the first of each month when the moon is full, a rider, bent over his mount's neck, sometimes can be seen thundering across the night sky. The mare, her coat shiny as pure copper and her mane and tail white as snow, fly wild in the wind. She runs on winged feet, stretching out to her fullest and leaving the stars behind. Suddenly she rears to a halt and a small figure leaps from the saddle, a pouch in his hand. As soon as his feet hit the ground, he disappears into the dust.

Camp Colorado was first established in 1856 along a creek north of the Colorado River to protect settlers in the area. A town grew up near the camp, named for Robert M. Coleman, aide-de-camp for Gen. Sam Houston.

Camp Colorado saw many attacks from Comanche Indians. The troops at Camp Colorado also established a mail route from Brownwood to Camp Colorado that continued to operate long after the fort was abandoned in the days following the Civil War. A young man who came to be known only as "Shorty" carried the mail from Brownwood to Coleman.

The man rode into Camp Colorado late one afternoon at a full gallop with several hostiles chasing him. The sergeant at the gate ordered his men to mount up, and they started after the Comanches.

Breathless, Shorty jumped off his horse and ran into the main building to deliver the mail and the payroll. He reported the race for his life to the officers, and that evening at the local saloon, he told his story again.

"If I wasn't so blamed short, them savages' arrows would've hit me square in the head. I suspect they never shot at a white man who was so short in the saddle. I just laid right down on Fancy's neck and let her fly." He gulped a shot of whiskey and ordered another.

"Don't know why they decided to chase me except they were wanting to get their hands on Fancy out there. She's the fastest horse around these parts, you know. Guess they didn't shoot low 'cause they were afraid of hitting her." He swilled down another whiskey, before speaking again.

"They could never catch her. My Fancy girl don't like the noise those rattlers make or that noise them Indians make when they're after a feller. That's probably what made her stretch out and run so fast. I'm telling you, boys, she brought tears to these eyes she ran so fast. Do you reckon if I was to wear me a hatband with a snake's rattler on it, she'd run fast all the time?"

Shorty accepted another glass and the slaps on the back from the crowd gathered around.

On each ride thereafter, he made sure to wear a hatband of snake rattlers to keep Fancy running. On their final mail run from Brownwood to Camp Colorado, Shorty and Fancy were riding along at a good crisp clip when a small band of Comanches came thundering toward them from Santa Anna Hill.

Shorty glanced up from the makings of a cigarette just in time to see the last pony reach the flat. Tossing his tobacco and paper to the wind, he gave Fancy her head and spurred her onward. The pair came within sight of the Camp Colorado stockade.

"Better get a move on it, Fancy, or they'll have our scalps on their lodge poles before nightfall." The rust-colored little mare twitched her ears and seemed to get a second burst of speed, but for only a few minutes. Shorty felt Fancy going down, but he wasn't quick enough to jump free. The sorrel mare stepped in a gopher hole and flipped over forward, breaking her neck in the fall. Death came instantly to Shorty as Fancy landed on top of him.

When Shorty and Fancy failed to appear at the appointed time with the mail, a detail of soldiers was sent out to look for them. Their bodies were found where they had fallen. Twenty or more war lances circled their corpses. The Indians had witnessed the demise of the rider and his horse and had honored them with the Comanche circle of protection. Shorty and Fancy were taken to the Camp Colorado cemetery, where they were buried together.

If you choose to pay your respects to Shorty and Fancy, take care where you step. You might tread on the grave of Rattlesnake Joe, purported to be the best snake charmer in West Texas. Joe lost his battle with a six-foot rattler in that cemetery, and he was laid to rest with the six-foot belly crawler that killed him.

Some folks claim to have heard the sound of a rattle while visiting the Camp Colorado cemetery. Joe worked at Camp Colorado as a scout on occasion. The rest of the time he hung around the fort looking for a handout.

Sometime before, he had fallen in love with a pretty young woman, but she chose to marry a man of financial means and broke Joe's heart. That's when Joe made his way to West Texas. Upon reaching Camp Colorado, he heard about an influx of rattlesnakes invading the countryside. A bounty was offered to anyone who could or would rid folks' homes and lands of the deadly snakes. The settlers posted the offer at Camp Colorado and Brownwood. Joe felt he had nothing to lose so he learned how to catch the poisonous snakes. Comanche Indians of the area ate the meat of the rattlers. The settlers found that the skins of the venomous snakes made good belts and decorations.

Joe sold his services and the snakes he caught to the highest bidder. Soon he had enough money to make a down payment on a nice farm and even thought about doing just that for a while. However, he reasoned that since he had no one to share it with, he might just as well spend his profits at a nearby saloon.

Spring and summer found Joe catching snakes. When winter set in, he went to work for the army as a scout. Indians considered Joe to be crazy for capturing the snakes. They stayed away from him because he was bad luck for them. This made him invaluable to the army and the settlers. With Joe around, the Indians would not attack.

Rattlesnake Joe drank too much and bragged too often that he would go out and catch a big rattler to make a whip for himself. One afternoon the intoxicated braggart left the fort. Joe never returned to Camp Colorado.

A patrol from Camp Colorado found his body three days later, with a six-foot rattler wrapped around his neck. It appeared Joe found the snake and tried to catch it before he killed it. It was a fight to the death between two West Texas warriors. The detail of

Coleman City Park is centered around the old stone administrator's building that has been relocated from Camp Colorado.

soldiers buried Rattlesnake Joe where they had found him, along with his opponent.

At three o'clock in the afternoon, Joe may be seen walking through the weeds near the cemetery. It is believed he is searching for an even bigger rattlesnake to prove his skills.

Stone by stone, the only remaining building of Camp Colorado was moved from private property where it once stood to the Coleman City Park. It is open for visitors to come inside, but the memorabilia is in the new museum in downtown Coleman at the Heritage Center, where the temperatures are controlled for the safekeeping of the papers and other items.

The cemetery with the headstones of the soldiers and settlers from the Coleman area who are buried there is all that is left of Camp Colorado. The crumbling headstones are so badly damaged there is no way to read who lies beneath them or when they died. The only visitors to the cemetery are the scorpions and wild animals of the West Texas range . . . and the rattlesnakes.

A concrete plaque marks the significance of the old administration building from short-lived Camp Colorado.

You can visit the cemetery with permission from the property owners, but be careful where you step. If you hear a rattler, beware. It could be the real thing or it might be Shorty wearing his rattling hatband. If not Shorty, perhaps the sound you hear is coming from Rattlesnake Joe's secret charm. Directions to the Camp Colorado Cemetery are available at the Camp Colorado Headquarters Building at the Coleman City Park, on US Highway 83/84 going south of Abilene, Texas.

FORT CIENEGA

After summer rains come to Cienega Creek, one lone Indian warrior can be seen around the Cienega Spring near where the Milton Faver family fort stood. The warrior's wife can be heard singing his death song out on the meadows, waiting to send him on his way to his heavenly home.

The rains from storm clouds drench the earth, and only the warrior's footprints are ever found. As the sun dries the ground, his footprints disappear, and his woman's tears are dried until the next rains fall.

Milton Faver came to the Cienega Creek, and he knew he would erect his fortress there because of the rain quenching the earth's surface, not the regular case in West Texas. Fort Cienega, built sometime between 1855 and 1857, had high walls and one-story flat-top adobe rooms. Not immune to Indian attacks, however, Cienega sported two square towers designed to provide defense on the southwest and northeast corners of the garrison.

Because the Indians could not breach the twenty-four-foot walls of Fort Cienega, they decided to tunnel under the wall to get inside. The Indians' plot was discovered, and Milton Faver and his men designed a surprise for the warriors while they worked to get into the stockade. The Indians dug through to the end of the tunnel into the interior of Fort Cienega, but the fight never really got started. The Indians didn't know what had hit them.

At the appearance of the first warrior from the hole in the ground, Faver shot and killed him, leaving no doubt to the remainder of his raiding party about the outcome of further fighting. Apparently, the other warriors turned and left immediately, abandoning their dead comrade where he fell.

When an Indian died, he would usually be taken back to his village, where the women prepared him for his final resting place with his favorite articles from life. His hunting knife, his bows and arrows, buffalo robes to keep him warm, his war paint, and sometimes his horse was killed and sent with him to carry him on his journey. Braves were not buried in the ground; they were placed on top of a scaffold to help them on their way to heaven.

Some say the dead warrior roams the grounds of the fort trapped inside the walls of Fort Cienega permanently. He can't find his way to heaven because his wife did not help him along on his long journey. Perhaps the brave is searching for his people, or maybe he searches for his favorite hunting items.

Fort Cienega, built as a family stronghold, served as an outpost for Fort Davis troops. During Civil War times, troops abandoned nearby Fort Davis and Indian attacks increased. Later, after Fort Davis was re-manned, Cienega served in a quasi-military-post capacity.

The Pool family bought Fort Cienega from the Faver descendants after Milton Faver passed away in 1889. When he passed away, ownership of the property was inherited by his son, Juan. Mr. John A. Pool bought the property from the Faver descendants, and by the end of the 1980s four generations of the Pool family had lived on the property.

Fort Cienega is located near the source of Cienega Creek about six miles east of Shafter, Texas, in central Presidio County, about thirty miles from Cíbolo Fort, and is currently part of Cíbolo Creek Ranch. According to the ranch's website, visitors can stay in one of several rooms either inside the fort or in an adjoining hacienda for a "historically authentic experience" while enjoying modern amenities.

FORT BELKNAP

Standing under the large trees that shade the grounds at Fort Belknap, I could almost hear the sound of reveille echo through the beautiful morning skies. Founded on June 24, 1851, by Bvt. Brig. Gen. William G. Belknap, Fort Belknap was a four-company post. Water supplied by springs found near the Brazos River kept the garrison alive. Jacals, small huts made of long poles chinked with clay and covered with thatched roofs, were built first. Later, these became obsolete and were replaced with stone buildings.

While visiting those stone buildings, I was told of many legends about Fort Belknap. One of the favorites was the one about two lovers: Elizabeth and a handsome young trooper named James.

On the morning of July 18, 1856, Elizabeth sat up in bed, happy to hear the bugler playing reveille. She sang a sweet ditty to the beat of the horses' hooves as they pranced across the parade grounds. Smiling lightly she listened to the soldiers' voices as they passed in front of the house on their way to breakfast. Then she sniffed the air for the smell of ham and eggs frying in her own

The ammunition storage building at Fort Belknap—known as one of the most beautiful forts in Texas—is in excellent condition.

kitchen. Elizabeth stepped out into the soft morning light and strolled to the large oak, where she sat on the ground to watch the sun rise.

Soldiers' shouts reverberated through the morning air. The sun peeked over the horizon and probed through the branches of the huge oak trees. Rays from the dawn shone on a figure waiting in the shadows. With her back against the trunk of the largest oak and an open locket in her hand, Elizabeth smiled upward at a tall, young soldier.

"James, I've been waiting for you. Where have you been?"

She rose to meet his embrace. Reaching up, she touched his face and swiped at a lock of blond curls hanging in his eyes. "I love you, James."

"And I love you, Elizabeth."

Their voices floated softly in the morning air.

He took her into his arms and whirled her around, her blue dimity gown swishing around her feet. He lifted her into the air until she squealed with delight.

"Let's not wait, Elizabeth." James set her back on the ground.

"Let's get married tomorrow. I am tired of waiting for the right time. I don't want to wait any longer." He kissed her, not waiting for her answer.

"Oh yes," she cried. "I don't want to wait, either."

"I'll talk to the chaplain when the officers' meeting is over." He took her in his arms and kissed her again. He then strolled off to his duties, whistling the wedding march softly.

She held the locket close to her chest and dreamily danced with joy, humming the same tune, but the shouting from the parade grounds interrupted her gaiety. Screams of terror filled the air quickly.

The peaceful morning was shattered by Kiowa war cries, striking panic among soldiers and civilians alike. Elizabeth ran through the crowd of milling people, painted savages, and frightened horses. She searched for James, but to no avail. Calling his name, she ran from one fallen soldier to another and looked into the staring eyes of death.

At last, she found her lover. Dropping to her knees she cradled James's body in her arms and wept. At the same time she held him close to her breast, an arrow pierced her heart and she slumped over the man she loved, dropping the tiny locket in the dirt.

A few people claim to have witnessed this death scene played out by the ghostly lovers on the dusty earth of the Fort Belknap parade grounds. They say it is like a mirage or even a movie reflected against the heat waves rising from the ground.

Companies posted at Fort Belknap through its years of service to the region included the Fifth US Infantry, the Second US Dragoons, the Seventh US Infantry, the Second US Cavalry, and the Sixth US Cavalry. The officers commanding these troops—Col. Gustavus Loomis, Maj. Enoch Steen, Captain Paul, Maj. George H. Thomas, Maj. Samuel Henry Starr, Lt. Col. Samuel Davis Sturgis, and Capt. Richard W. Johnson—demanded much respect for their expertise as leaders.

The water well at Fort Belknap

Being the northernmost anchor in the chain of forts protecting Texas and the frontier, Fort Belknap stood firm for many years. Its troops patrolled from the Red River to the Rio Grande, yet Fort Belknap survived without the defensive works most encampments of this era offered. The troops sometimes went out on raids against the Indians that threatened the area, traveling as far as the northern Kansas border. However, there were a few occasions of attack at the fort itself. The hub of roads stretched in every direction, and Fort Belknap was a stop on the Butterfield Overland Mail route leading to San Francisco.

On February 9, 1861, federal troops had been removed from the fort in preparation for war and it was surrendered. The fort was later abandoned but reoccupied by state troops and then later by the US Calvary in 1867.

A grape arbor planted after World War I covers part of the parade grounds where Elizabeth and James sometimes met.

In 1936, the state, using supplemental federal funds, began restoring the fort. At the time, only the magazine and part of the corn house were still standing. The state restored these structures and reconstructed the commissary, a kitchen, two two-story barracks, and the well. All of the buildings of the fort are on the original foundations except the kitchen, constructed between the barracks. The buildings are made of stone with shingled roofs.

The twenty-acre site then became a county park. The site was designated as a National Historic Landmark in 1960.

Today, the Fort Belknap Society has museums in the commissary and corn house. In partnership with Texas Wesleyan College, the Fort Belknap Archives of Western America is located in one of the barracks. One of the former infantry barracks is being used as a community center. In the town of Belknap is a monument to Indian agent Robert Neighbors. Robert Simpson Neighbors was an Indian agent as well as a renowned Texas state legislator. He was a fair and determined protector of Indian interests. He made sure that things went according to the treaties with the Indians. However, sadly, he was murdered for his beliefs about the Indians by a Texas citizen who disagreed with giving any rights to the Comanches or any other Indian.

The fort is located in Young County, on State Highway 251, about three miles south of Newcastle. The Fort Belknap Cemetery is also available for viewing across the highway from the fort compound.

FORT BLISS

More than a few ghosts reside at Fort Bliss, and the most predominant story is the one of a retired cavalry sergeant. The army had been his life since he was a youth. He fought in many skirmishes and was applauded for his bravery and excellent leadership until a superior officer accused him of negligence of duty. He was forced into a retirement that weighed heavily on his shoulders.

He has been seen walking the halls of the same building, and he moves in and out of the courtroom doors, which appear to swing open and shut at will.

The sergeant's body had been laid to rest in the old morgue for a few days before he was buried. The morgue building at Fort Bliss, one of the oldest buildings on the grounds, has visitors day and night from another era. A bearded cavalryman, along with other men and women, has been seen in the morgue's windows and walking the halls. If anyone approaches the building, the shadows fade into the lonely darkness within.

Singing in the old theater can be heard as a young woman's gravelly voice belts out a bawdy song from the stage. Performances are put on for anyone who believes and will listen. The old building was once referred to as being the "Tumbleweed Tavern," where the soldiers and settlers went to enjoy the songs of skimpily clad women of the evening. The structure is now called the MacGregor Range/Asa P. Grey Recreation Center.

In November 1848 six rifle companies of the Third Infantry regiment established Fort Bliss at El Paso del Norte. It was earlier known by the name "The Post Opposite El Paso" and eventually was relocated and renamed Fort Bliss. On March 8, 1854, the assistant adjutant general during the Mexican War, Lt. Col. William Wallace Smith Bliss, was honored by having the fort officially named for him.

Fort Bliss had to be moved and rebuilt several times between the 1860s and the 1870s. With the coming of the railroad in the 1880s, Fort Bliss and El Paso were quickly industrialized.

In 1890 seven railroads converged on El Paso and Fort Bliss. Five of these were American and two were Mexican, and this made El Paso a vital commercial center for distribution of goods. The army decided to make Fort Bliss the major fort in the region, and with the help of the El Paso citizenry, the army relocated it onto 1,266 acres of the Lanoria Mesa, where it remains today.

It took two years to rebuild Fort Bliss on the mesa. Capt. George Ruhlen designed the layout, which was centered around a parade ground situated on the curve of the mesa.

When the revolution broke out in Mexico, the US Army reinforced the manpower at Fort Bliss with cavalry, infantry, and

A replica of historic Fort Bliss WIKIMEDIA COMMONS

artillery troops. These troops guarded every entrance into the United States from Mexico.

In 1911 the War Department decided to convert Fort Bliss to a cavalry post. After General Pershing's failure to capture Pancho Villa in 1916, Fort Bliss was used as a training-and-drilling exercise post. It gave the army opportunities to conduct much-needed military maneuvers on a larger scale, before the country's entry into World War I in 1917.

Although not used much in World War I, the cavalry units were still the best and most effective way to patrol the border between the United States and Mexico.

When the war in Europe ended, Pancho Villa began harassing US citizens, and the army turned its focus on the borders once more. On June 16, 1919, Fort Bliss received eighteen airplanes to use for border patrol. The airplanes' runways had previously been cavalry drill fields.

Between the world wars, the horse cavalry in the nation went into decline. Although the army used airplanes and other machinery at Fort Bliss, the mounted troops continued to patrol the borders. The Seventh and Eighth Cavalry Regiments were assigned separate cantonments in 1919 and 1920.

The cavalry units were deactivated in 1921, and the army incorporated the Seventh and Eighth Cavalry Regiments into the First Cavalry Division. It never really achieved its fullest strength potential, but the First Cavalry Division succeeded in transforming Fort Bliss into the nation's number one cavalry installation.

The United States entered World War II in 1941, and Fort Bliss housed the largest horse cavalry force in the nation. However, the need for the horse cavalry was lessened in 1942 when Mexico declared war on the Axis powers.

The War Department discontinued the horse cavalry in 1943 at Fort Bliss and converted the First Cavalry Division into a mechanized unit with infantry for the Pacific theater.

Some people wonder how the cavalry soldier who hanged himself would feel about the Fort Bliss of today. The fort began its transformation into the nation's largest antiaircraft artillery training center in 1943. Now the base comprises 1.1 million acres of land stretching across the western tip of Texas into New Mexico. The Fort Bliss Cemetery is the site of over 43,000 graves of US soldiers.

Visit El Paso, Texas, and Fort Bliss simultaneously. Fort Bliss surrounds the city of El Paso.

FORT STOCKTON

"El Bulto! Help me! It's El Bulto!"

The cry went up and all strained to see the black-clad figure disappearing into the alleyway.

The sheriff hitched up his britches. "Now, we've got him. Come on, Mack. Let's get rid of this pervert before he scares the daylights out of anybody else."

The two officers followed the man into the dead-end alley. Carefully checking behind the crates and boxes scattered in the darkened area, the officers shone their flashlight beams here and there to aid in their search. Quickly they reached the end of the alley.

"I don't know how he does it, Mack, but he got away again. There's no one back here."

At his last words, the officers heard a rumbling laughter in the darkness above them.

Quickly shining their beams upward, the officers' mouths dropped open at the sight. El Bulto floated above them, laughing before instantly fading into nothingness.

One of the most prominent spirit figures haunting the old sutlery at Fort Stockton is that of a large man dressed entirely in black. The description is always the same, although no one has seen his face.

Sightings have been reported to the police many times. These reports are never shrugged off or deemed fanciful. There are officers, dispatchers, local residents, and passersby who have observed the darkly clad apparition.

Many folks believe that the dark figure is George "Choche" Garcia, who apparently lived in the old adobe sutlery sometime between the 1930s and 1950s when he experimented with marijuana. He was said to have begun dressing in black and going out to scare the citizens.

Some say the ghostly being is Barney Riggs, who in 1902 beat his wife, Maria, before burning all their possessions. He later threatened to douse her in kerosene and set fire to her. She fled his outrage and sought refuge with Matilde Pina, who lived in the old sutlery. Barney's stepson shot him on the steps of the sutlery, killing him, when he came looking for Maria.

In 1918, the Spanish flu epidemic hit Fort Stockton, and the old building was used as a hospital. A yellow flag warning people of contagion flew over it for many weeks. The folks who contracted the disease and died at the former sutlery were buried behind the building in a deep natural draw out back.

Other rumors of the dark ghost come from the fact that the old sutlery was once used as a frontier courthouse. The guilty parties were hanged from a large tree behind the building. Others believe the identity of the apparition is Pancho Robles. He supposedly practiced witchcraft in the old adobe building at night and was consumed by his witching idolaters.

Apparently the ghost isn't afraid of anything or anyone. He appears whenever he pleases.

Reports of this big bold ghost have been widespread over the years. The claims vary from flickering lights within the vacant building, to the sound of china being shattered. The noises have been investigated, but no trace of broken china can be found. There is no one to turn the lights off and on.

Fort Stockton was first manned in December 1858, but it was not formally established until March 1859. It was temporarily abandoned in 1861 when the Civil War broke out. Southern troops manned the post briefly until they withdrew in 1862 to serve in the war.

In July 1867 the fort was re-established with four companies of soldiers, 75 percent of which were Buffalo Soldiers. Permanent abandonment came in June 1886, when Fort Stockton was no longer considered to be necessary by the army.

The Fort Stockton State Historic Site is located in Fort Stockton, along Interstate 10, approximately 321 miles west of San Antonio. Fort Stockton is 243 miles east of El Paso, 87 miles south-southwest of Odessa on Interstate 20, and 53 miles from Pecos on US Highway 285.

FORT McINTOSH

During its active tenure from 1849 to 1947, Fort McIntosh was the longest continually garrisoned fort in Texas history, carrying a load on its historic shoulders. Sometimes the load became heavier than at other times.

Lt. Egbert Ludovicus Viele, who in later years designed Central Park in New York City, was dispatched from Fort Ringgold to Fort McIntosh with a company of the First US Infantry. Other notable officers, including Philip H. Sheridan and Randolph B. Marcy, commanded troops from Fort McIntosh. Texas Ranger John S. Ford brought yet another company of troops to the Rio Grande fort.

Built adjacent to the river ford known as Indian Crossing, Fort McIntosh saw its share of attacks from the tribes in the area. After the first withdrawal of troops in 1859, the local economy became badly depressed. The fort saw a re-garrison, and the original earthwork fort was rebuilt by army engineers and troop labor. The fort was built in the shape of a star and perched on a bluff overlooking the Rio Grande. At first called Camp Crawford, Fort McIntosh was renamed for Lt. Col. James S. McIntosh, who died on September 26, 1847, from wounds received in the battle of Molino Del Rey.

Abandoned in March 1859, Fort McIntosh was later reoccupied in January 1860 and again abandoned in April 1861 due to the troops leaving to fight the Civil War. Eventually it was reopened after the Civil War in 1865. Until the 1880s Fort McIntosh soldiers were involved in escort duty and scouting.

Several unsuccessful Union attacks were launched on Fort McIntosh during the Civil War while the Confederate soldiers defended the post. After the Civil War federal troops finished the permanent structures of the fort.

In 1899, an incident occurred that brought notoriety and public outcry from local citizens, when several black troops went into nearby Laredo to enjoy a night away from the fort. The citizens of the city, nervous because of their presence at Fort McIntosh, had requested more police protection from the city managers.

Police officers were instructed to stop every black soldier or private citizen for questioning. One officer, doing the job assigned to him, stopped the group from the fort. The officer asked where they were going, where they'd been, and how long they would be in the city.

According to what has been told, the black troops, not liking the idea of being questioned or harassed, took offense to the officer's questions and bludgeoned him to death. Some claim they've seen this violent act played out on a dark night at the fort grounds, but the body of the beaten officer disappears before anyone can come to his assistance.

Because of the troops' behavior, the citizens demanded the entire removal of black troops from Texas. Governor Joseph Sayers had the men involved with the murder arrested, and the citizens began to calm, especially when they thought Washington might possibly close Fort McIntosh.

Many years later, Fort McIntosh served as a training camp for World War I and World War II soldiers. After ninety-eight years of service, Fort McIntosh officially closed in 1946.

A marker for Fort McIntosh is set at the front gate of Laredo College. There are still some buildings from Fort McIntosh in use at the Laredo-Washington Street entrance to the city. You can reach these buildings by driving along Interstate 35 in San Antonio, from State Highway 359 in Miranda City, or even off US Highway 59 out of Freer.

Through the years, many modern buildings, designed to incorporate the latest in technology and design, have been added. The latest addition, the De la Garza Building with its sunburst windows, offers us a look at the site's past as a fort looking out toward the river. Much as the Indians and Spaniards did, we do not see a boundary, but a bridge to the future.

FORT LANCASTER

Fort Lancaster first became established on the banks of Live Oak Creek on August 29, 1855, to protect the lower San Antonio to El Paso Road in the years after the discovery of gold in the California mountains. In August 1859 the Butterfield Overland Mail changed routes west from the upper to the lower road. Three coaches per month ran past Fort Lancaster.

On a particularly hot summer evening in 1860, while escorting a coach carrying the mail, the detachment of troops and the coach were attacked. One young trooper, Corporal Hanes, scheduled to be re-stationed in a few weeks, received a flesh wound in the leg. Hanes insisted he could still ride and fight, but his commanding officer ordered him inside the mail coach. Being a good soldier, Hanes followed orders and settled into the vehicle.

The Mescalero Apaches attacked again and again. They came in waves. Ten to twelve braves came at the detachment on the first run. After drawing some of the soldiers away from the coach, another group of similar size sat waiting farther down the route.

When the second wave of warriors hit, they used burning arrows and attacked the coach, setting it ablaze. They left immediately, drawing more soldiers away from the mail and payroll in the coach.

The troops in the detachment left the coach driver and the corporal to their own defenses. The Mescaleros struck the coach with another wave of battle-ready braves. The driver was shot and killed, and the horses bolted out of control. Corporal Hanes was alone in the runaway coach as it rolled across the prairie, engulfed in flames. When the tongue of the wagon broke, the coach overturned and Corporal Hanes crawled out, his clothes on fire. He held his hands up to the heavens and limped away from the burning coach before one of the Indians shot him through the heart with a burning arrow. This ended one of the worst incidents in the command of Captain Carpenter at Fort Lancaster.

Capt. Stephen D. Carpenter commanded Companies H and K of the First US Infantry when the fort was first established. Command switched between Captain Carpenter and Capt. R. S. Granger several times between February 1856 and 1861, when Texas seceded from the Union.

Men stationed at the fort escorted mail and freight trains for those going west. Keeping vigil, the troops pursued the Mescalero Apaches and Comanches as they patrolled their segment of the road.

Originally the soldiers constructed the fort of pickets, canvas, and portable Turnley prefabricated buildings; however, before the army abandoned Fort Lancaster for the Civil War, the buildings were reconstructed of stone and adobe.

After the Civil War broke out, Walter P. Lane's rangers occupied Fort Lancaster from December 1861 to April 1862. These men soon became a part of Company F, of the Second Regiment of the Texas Mounted Rifles. In 1871 Fort Lancaster became a subpost for a company of infantry and a cavalry detachment.

The army abandoned the post in late 1873 or early 1874. Most of its buildings were torn down and used in building the nearby town of Sheffield, Texas.

Today, visitors wander through ruins imagining the once-impressive establishment of twenty-five permanent buildings—including a blacksmith shop, hospital, sutler's store, and bakery—and enjoy the sights, sounds, and wildlife of West Texas.

Hours of operation are from 9:00 a.m. to 5:00 p.m. daily except Thanksgiving Day, Christmas Eve, Christmas Day, New Year's Eve, and New Year's Day. Admissions fees are as follows: adults: four dollars; adult group tour: three dollars per person; ages six to eighteen: three dollars per person; ages five and younger: free; school groups: one dollar per student. Reservations are required for group tours.

To visit Fort Lancaster's ruins, drive eight miles east of Sheffield on Interstate 10. Take exit 343 and follow US Highway 290 to the park. If you're there on a hot summer day, through the heat waves bouncing off the pavement you just might see a uniformed figure with arms stretching upward walking silently out of a fiery ring of smoke, clothes ablaze. The figure limps while moving forward and then fades into the shimmering air with his arms still outstretched.

FORT CLARK

While on a reconnaissance mission for the War Department, W. H. C. Whiting recognized the military potential of a site long favored by the Comanches, the Lipan Apaches, the Mescaleros, and other tribes. He recommended that the War Department raise a fort on the big Las Mores Springs where the great Comanche Trail led into Mexico on the eastern branch of the creek.

On June 20, 1852, Maj. Joseph H. LaMotte, commanding two companies of the First Infantry and an advance and rear guard of the US Mounted Rifles, later known as the Third Cavalry, established Fort Clark at the site Whiting had chosen. Originally, the

Fort Clark commissary WIKIMEDIA COMMONS

fort carried the name Fort Riley. At Major Riley's insistence, however, Lt. Col. D. C. Tompkins changed the name to Fort Clark on July 20, 1852.

Federal soldiers left Fort Clark on March 19, 1861, with the Civil War on the horizon, but the Second Texas Mounted Rifles stayed until August 1862. Between the time federal troops left in 1861 and the reoccupation on December 12, 1866, Fort Clark served the Confederate troops. They used the fort for a supply depot and hospital for themselves and civilians in the area.

The Seminole-Negro Indian Scouts served at the fort from 1872 until 1914. Lt. John L. Bullis commanded these scouts between 1873 and 1881. At one time Fort Clark served as headquarters for Col. Ranald Mackenzie's raids into Mexico. Mackenzie and his troops were instrumental in stopping the raiding, killing, and stealing perpetrated by Indians and bandits who crossed the border to safety.

In 1873, Colonel Mackenzie, Lieutenant Bullis, and the Seminole-Negro Indian Scouts led a patrol into Mexico in pursuit of the Lipan Apaches for attacks against the settlers of the Fort

Clark district. Again in 1878 Mackenzie, Bullis, and the Indian scouts along with a large peacetime army crossed the Rio Grande to put an end to the Indian fighting forever. The last Indian attacks in the Nueces District occurred in 1881.

Most of the infantry units and the cavalry units of the army were at one time stationed at Fort Clark. The Ninth and Tenth Black Buffalo Soldiers were there, as well. With no more Indian wars, the army threatened Fort Clark with closure, but the Mexican revolutionaries made it necessary to re-garrison the post. The fort was used again when World War I broke out in Europe. In 1941, the Fifth Cavalry transferred from Fort Clark to Fort Bliss. The 112th Cavalry of the Texas National Guard then manned Fort Clark until they could be shipped out for combat in the Pacific. Some twelve thousand troops trained and waited for deployment from Fort Clark in February 1944.

After the end of World War II, Fort Clark officially closed in 1946 because the fully mechanized army had no more use for one of the last horse-cavalry posts in the nation.

Later that same year the Brown and Root Company bought Fort Clark for salvage, and at one time they used it for a guest ranch.

The ghost of an orderly, once assigned to live with an officer's family, is reportedly still carrying out his duties in one of the houses on Colony Row. On occasion, residents claim to be awakened around 4:00 a.m. by the smell of breakfast being prepared. The aroma of frying bacon or sausage and hot biscuits blends with the smell of hot coffee to fill the area.

Several visitors have told about staying overnight at the houses of certain residents and becoming curious as to who did the cooking at such an early hour. Each guest told of going from room to room but finding no one. A few reported hearing the sound of a soft sigh, although they could not detect the source.

Another visitor, Grace Bennett, tells the story of her sister, who once visited the fort. According to Grace, she had dropped an earring and it had rolled under the bed. The earrings belonged to her sister, and Grace had no choice but to get down on the floor and fish it out. When she got down on her hands and knees, something or someone grabbed her foot and tugged on it. Thinking her friend might be playing a trick on her, Grace kicked out gently, but the tugging continued. She looked around to see who kept pulling on her, but she saw no one. She was alone in the room.

Some believe the spirit of Ollabelle Dahlastrom, who once owned and lived in one of the houses at Fort Clark, is still present. Perhaps she is taking care of unfinished business or, as one known for her humor, is up to her old tricks.

Other visitors claim to feel the presence of an army wife and heard faint music in the house where Mrs. Dahlastrom lived. The wife, being left alone much of the time, spent hours at her most treasured possession: a beautiful rosewood piano. There has been some debate as to the proper title to the song heard, but several agree the tune is "Beautiful Dreamer."

Other stories have emerged from Colony Row, ranging from the sad to the mischievous. At another house, a woman cries out in the night for a baby who is ill or may be dying. Then her vapory figure turns with arms outstretched, as if pleading, while the faint wail of a baby echoes in the background.

Obviously, one of the spirits still retains its mischievous nature. One older gentleman claims someone shook his bed in the night, nearly dumping him onto the floor. Later, in the same room, another occupant complained about his blankets being pulled to the bottom of the bed. Several other incidents involved pictures being moved from place to place and jewelry disappearing and then showing up in unlikely places. Brass candleholders have been taken off the wall in one lady's home and tossed across the room. Although they hit the floor, there has never been any damage to the candlesticks.

Many visitors have found the episodes amusing while a few found them frightening and will never return to Fort Clark. I prefer to believe this is the spirit of a child, a child whose time was cut short.

In 1971, the property of Fort Clark became part of the Fort Clark Springs Association, which has developed the area, providing not only a living and resort community, but also preserving eighty buildings and designating the area as a National Register Historic District. The old cavalry barracks have been transformed into a hotel. The old guardhouse is a museum now, operated by the Fort Clark Historical Society. It is open on weekends.

Today, twenty-five to thirty buildings dating from the nineteenth century survive, including two sets of officers' quarters and another log building, which dates from the early 1850s. Other buildings, constructed of stone, were built from the late 1850s to the 1880s. These include officers' quarters, barracks, the commanding officer's house, quartermaster storehouse, and guardhouse.

Called Fort Clark Springs today, the old fort site is a privately owned resort and leisure living community. However, its being a commercial endeavor has only helped in the preservation of this historic fort. The resort includes an 18-hole golf course, and the old Fort Clark spring feeds a natural swimming pool. Camping and RV sites are available. Fort Clark Springs is located at the southern edge of Brackettville, Texas.

Visitors are welcomed by volunteer hosts to the Old Fort Clark Guardhouse Museum in Kinney County at Brackettville on US Highway 90 west of Uvalde.

FORT LINCOLN

Fort Lincoln was established on the banks of Seco Creek on July 7, 1849, at the same site where a company of Texas Rangers had camped the year before. The 1,476 acres had been deeded to the heirs of Milton Anderson on August 27, 1846. The fort was built on open ground to provide a commanding view of the area.

At that time, Maj. James Longstreet commanded Companies E and G of the Eighth US Infantry. Second in command was Lt.

Richard Irving Dodge, for whom Dodge City, Kansas, was named. These officers were stationed at Fort Lincoln to track down Indians who raided the settlers and to protect properties and human life on the Woll Road. Woll Road was the most important trade route from San Antonio to Fort Duncan and other western points.

In 1851, Fort Lincoln's barracks, used by the two companies of infantry, were made of gray limestone. Several temporary buildings were constructed of logs and poles with shingle, thatch, or tarp roofs.

On July 20, 1852, Fort Lincoln was abandoned by the military, but rangers made use of the buildings for a time. Soon after the rangers were gone, the barracks were torn down and used to construct residences for nearby settlers. Water for the fort had been hauled up from the creek, which was no more than a few standing pools of spring-fed water.

Hauling water was one of the most boring, backbreaking details in the whole army, but Corporal Allen didn't mind. He performed his duty with a smile and never complained. After all, he had hauled many a barrel of water in his lifetime. Living on a farm sometimes meant doing things you didn't really want to do, but his parents taught him to make the best of a bad or hard situation.

One day while filling the water barrels, he saw a young Indian maiden washing her hair in the creek. He stared, puzzled and a little afraid. When she rose from the water, several women surrounded her. The women seemed to have no substance other than mist. The girl floated through the nearby brush and disappeared. He followed along the path and heard wails of pain and suffering.

Fearfully, Corporal Allen crept forward to a small clearing in a grove of trees. In the center of the clearing he found a bloodied deerskin dress—all that remained of the maiden. Floating above the dress was a circle of mist.

Allen rushed back and finished filling the barrels to haul back to the fort. When he arrived at the fort, he sought out the Indian scout Half Moon and began asking questions about the Indian girl.

"Half Moon, you must help me." Corporal Allen described the scene from the stream. "What could be going on? Where did the girl go?"

"I don't know, Corporal. I have no knowledge of anyone as you describe." Half Moon insisted he knew nothing about a maiden in the area. Corporal Allen watched the man's face closely and knew Half Moon was lying.

"You will go with me to where I saw the girl last. I'll tell the sergeant."

"I do not wish to go with you to this place."

"You will go with me, or I'll tell the sergeant about that bottle of whiskey you carry with you all the time. You know you aren't supposed to drink that stuff, and Sarge will be plenty mad at you for having it."

The next trip Allen made for water, he took the scout along.

Again the maiden was seen bathing in the creek and disappeared in the same spot.

Allen pointed to the shrouded maiden. "See, there she is. Who is she?"

A frightened look flashed in Half Moon's eyes, and he started to run. "I don't know who or what she is. I'm leaving!"

Allen caught the scout's arm and pulled him back. "No, we're going to find her—now."

Forcing a terrified Half Moon to go along, he found only the dress again, the bloodstains standing out against the beautiful decorations on the deerskin.

Half Moon gasped and backed away. "I will not stay here any longer."

Allen caught his arm and held him fast. He demanded Half Moon tell him what had happened.

Half Moon struggled to speak, but no words came. He pulled away from Allen and ran back to the fort, leaving Allen to fill the barrels.

That evening Allen dreamed of the young maiden. She came

to him in a gossamer-clouded mist. In his dream he heard her warning, "Do not come back to the water's edge."

The next morning he tried to find Half Moon, but the scout was nowhere to be found. A further search showed he had packed his belongings and left the fort during the night. Allen saddled his horse and rode out toward the creek where he had first seen the girl. Hoping for one more glance, he stepped off his horse and waited for hours, pacing the bank of the creek. The sun's warmth and the sound of the water rolling over the rocks nearly lulled him to sleep until bloodcurdling screams of agony pierced the air.

Jumping up, Allen ran toward the sounds and then fell to his knees, horrified at the scene before him. Half Moon was hanging by his feet from a tree limb. Blood ran in rivulets from the scout's slashed throat and dripped onto the deerskin dress lying below.

As Allen watched, a cloud of mist retreated into the brush. When he could move again, he cut Half Moon's body from the tree. He tried to piece the events together, to make sense of what he had seen, but to no avail.

He carried Half Moon and the dress back to the fort, where he talked to an old Indian woman who worked as a laundress for the soldiers.

"The dress is the ceremonial marriage dress of a chief's daughter." The woman pointed to the beadwork on the front. "This tells of a marriage match between the chief's daughter and a great warrior. He is a strong well-placed man in the tribe. Where did you get the dress? Why are there bloodstains on it?"

He related his story about the maiden and Half Moon's grisly murder. As he spoke, he watched the woman's eyes, searching for the truth.

"Then Half Moon was the guilty party." With these words, she spat on the ground in front of Allen's boots.

"Guilty of what?"

"Half Moon has been punished for raping and killing a chief's daughter, a maiden promised to a brave warrior."

Allen now knew why the girl's spirit had come to him. She wanted him to help her avenge her shame and her death.

He certainly didn't condone the actions taken against the scout, and he wondered if he should report it to his commanding officer. He felt that justice had been served, but then he couldn't tell anyone a ghost did this to Half Moon.

If he reported what he had heard he knew other Indians would be accused of the crime. The army and their officers had no regard for Indians' lives, and they would be hunted down and killed. Allen decided not to report the incident.

He did what he thought was best. He took Half Moon's body back to where he found it and left it there. Then he returned to the place where he first saw the young girl's misty form in the water. He waited for a while. Convinced she was finished with him and would not return, he mounted his horse and started back to his quarters.

He reined his horse around for one last look, and as he did he saw the maiden standing at the water's edge in her marriage garment.

She smiled and shyly waved before slowly walking into the brush, where she disappeared forever. The Indian maiden has not been seen since Corporal Allen helped her avenge her death. His story was related through the years as one of my grandpa's yarns.

Soon after the fort was abandoned, Richard Reily, an Irishman, bought the old fort and used the hospital as his home. Unfortunately, none of the buildings remain, and there is only a marker to prove that military personnel and Indians were ever there.

Rocks from the buildings were used for residences in D'Hanis. Today there are only remnants of a structure left of the fort. Sometime in 1936 a Texas Centennial Marker was erected. To see the ruins of Fort Lincoln, follow FM 1796 two miles north out of D'Hanis and then take a left onto County Road 4204. What's left of the fort is next to Seco Creek, on private property with a No Trespassing sign.

CAMP HUDSON

Camp Hudson troops in the 1850s, 1860s, and 1870s were primarily used for escorting settlers and the mail coaches traveling along the Chihuahua Trail.

On June 7, 1857, Camp Hudson was one in a line of forts built along the mail route between San Antonio and El Paso. Perched on one of the most isolated sections of San Pedro Creek, the post rarely had visitors other than army personnel or Indians.

Camp Hudson boasted buildings made of a mixture of gravel and lime that were warm in the winter and cool in the summer. Although it was a slow building process, it was well worth it when the structures were finally finished.

Camp Hudson residents, mostly army personnel, built and opened a post office shortly after the fort was established on June 7, 1857. Troops left Camp Hudson on March 17, 1861, because of the Civil War. The post office closed in 1866 and was not reopened. Troops were not stationed again at Camp Hudson until November 1867, a month after a stage was ambushed and its military escorts murdered by the Mescaleros in a bloody battle.

"What is today, Bert?"

"October 27, I think. Ain't real sure. Don't keep up with it much." Both men became quiet again.

The mail stage bounced along the dusty Chihuahua Trail while the team of six horses pulled the coach through the warm October wind.

Several miles later, Sam spoke. "Sure glad them army boys are back there to lend a hand if there's any trouble." Sam spit a stream of tobacco juice to the ground.

"Yep, it didn't hurt my feelings none either when the old man told me he was going to get them to tag along. I hate this stretch of the route." Bert slapped the reins on the horses' backs. "Get on up there. Don't know why the old man don't get some better horses, especially old Red down there. He's sure lazy and causes the others to have to work way harder than they should."

"Yeah, sometimes I think them yahoos back there in the East ought to have to live and work out here some, so they'd know how things are and wouldn't be so danged stingy with supplies and payroll."

Tobacco juice flew, splattering over the side of the coach.

"Good thing we don't have passengers today." Sam shaded his eyes from the sun and looked out across the desert-like horizon. "Holy smoke! You better whip old Red's fanny and make him pick up the pace a whole lot more. Here comes a passel of those Mescaleros."

Bert cracked his whip over the horses' heads, urging them on. Sam stood up on the seat and motioned to the sergeant leading the troops about the trouble coming toward them.

The sergeant rode up alongside the stage. "What's wrong?"

Sam pointed to the cloud of dust rolling along the prairie. "Them is Mescaleros. They done heard about this big payroll back there in the boot, and they want it to buy rifles from the Mexicans, no doubt."

"We'll take care of them. Keep on to Fort Stockton."

Tobacco Sam spat at the ground. "Like we was going to stop and watch him play with the Indians."

"Better get your rifle ready to fire, Sam." Bert alternately watched the road and the Indians.

The war party grew closer. He cracked the whip louder.

When the stage careened around the base of a hill, a hundred or more warriors wasted no time in riddling the coach and the two men with bullets. Sam slumped on the seat and watched helplessly as Bert fell to the ground. He kept still while an Indian climbed up on the wheel and started to toss him off the coach. Tobacco Sam forced one last mouthful of tobacco juice between his teeth and spit it into the warrior's eyes. Sam grinned at the yelling warrior. The Indian jumped off the stage and went rolling in the dirt.

Another warrior rode close to the mail coach and shot Sam through the heart.

The ambush of the stage and its escorts drew attention from Washington, and within a month Camp Hudson was re-garrisoned once more.

Companies D and G of the Ninth Cavalry immediately reoccupied Camp Hudson after this attack, and by April 1868 other troops accompanied them. In April 1871 Camp Hudson thrived under the command of three commissioned officers and sixty or more enlisted men.

January 1877 brought a halt to the threat of Indian attack to the few settlers, and Camp Hudson was closed.

When my friend and I visited Camp Hudson, I talked to several people who had seen ghostly riders out on the desert, so I drove out to the spot most of them told me about.

Heat waves rose off the scorched earth on the Chihuahua Trail. The blinding sun was horrible on the lonely stretch of road. We were talking as I drove along and suddenly I had to slam on my brakes to avoid hitting a man in a blue 1800s army uniform riding his horse across the highway.

"What's the matter with you?" my friend Sammy asked.

"Didn't you see that man?"

"Nope, sure didn't. You are believing too much of what you hear."

Sammy and I stepped out of the vehicle, and I watched the man on the horse smile and wave at me and then disappear into the heat waves.

"You didn't see that either, I suppose?"

"Nope, I didn't. I never see them. Why won't the ghosts appear to me, too?"

I shook my head and rubbed my eyes. Sammy and I decided that I should walk around a bit to refresh myself and so that maybe she could see the man, too. I glanced out across the desert terrain and again saw the man on the horse, dust kicking up behind them before they disappeared as quickly as they appeared, and just as I started to tell Sammy they were there again, they were gone.

Exasperated, I climbed back in the car. "Let's get out of here before I lose my mind." When we arrived at the hotel that evening, I talked to several people at the restaurant and acquired a few more facts and several confirmations that I was not the only one to see the roaming soldier.

In 1936, the Texas Historical Commission placed a centennial marker at the site of Camp Hudson. By the 1980s no buildings stood on the private property where the camp was once situated. The site is located in a desolate rock-strewn field. A state marker and a small gravestone are all that's left of the old post. The site is located in Val Verde County, on State Highway 163, about twenty miles north of Comstock.

FORT QUITMAN

Boredom is a curse to some, but to others, who can create their own entertainment, boredom is merely a challenge. Building fence can be a ho-hum job, especially if you are working alone on a line that is a mile or so long. Riding the range, looking for one old cow that dropped a calf and has hidden it out somewhere on five hundred or more acres is boring work, too. These sorts of jobs down near McNary usually summon up company from out of nowhere, and there are times when a certain sergeant from Fort Quitman appears to the lonely cowboys on the trail.

Sergeant Tom is usually smiling broadly, carrying a length of rope, and if the man on watch is receptive, the Sarge will begin jumping that rope. Reports from a specific cowboy who was on night watch over a small herd of cattle says that the sergeant "jumped that darned rope for about an hour one night, darn near putting me to sleep counting how many times he jumped it." When the cowboy quit counting, Sergeant Tom faded into the night, and the cowboy hasn't seen him since.

A description of Fort Quitman and one of its soldiers by Lydia Spencer Lane, who was visiting the fort at the time, didn't make the fort or the soldier famous. Many more folks other than Miss

Lane, however, have seen that particular soldier since that fateful day she watched him.

Lydia Lane wrote, "I was surprised to see a sergeant dressed in full dress uniform jumping rope outside the guardhouse. If anyone at Fort Quitman could feel cheerful enough to enjoy so innocent a pastime in such a forlorn and tumble-down place, he is to be commended." Comments from fort surgeon John J. Culver weren't nearly as nice. He reported that the establishment was "entirely unworthy of the name fort, post, or station for United States troops."

All supplies were hauled in from San Elizario, El Paso, or San Ignacio, Chihuahua. None of the buildings had doors or windows, and few even had roofs. The soldiers were continually making repairs on the barracks for the two companies of men. The ground was so poor a garden would wilt away to nothingness.

According to legends, on the morning of Sergeant Tom's death, he was sitting in front of the guardhouse dozing. The captive Indians inside mumbled quietly.

Sergeant Tom took a deep breath and inhaled the aroma of breakfast and hot coffee being prepared. Stretching to the sky, he stood and looked around at the activity on the fort grounds. He wished his replacement would hurry and get to his post. The sergeant picked up his length of rope and started jumping again. Suddenly his rope was jerked out of his hands and wrapped around his neck. The Indians inside the guardhouse pulled the rope tight. One of the captives reached into the sergeant's coat pocket and pulled out the key. Another pulled the rope taut; putting enough pressure on it to crush Sergeant Tom's windpipe, and the trooper fell to the ground in a lifeless heap. When the replacement guard arrived, Sergeant Tom was dead and the guardhouse was empty.

Fort Quitman was established only four hundred yards east of the Rio Grande and officially manned on September 28, 1858, by Capt. Arthur T. Lee and Companies C and H of the Eighth Infantry. Quitman was to help protect travelers and the mail stage from San Antonio to El Paso, a task not easily carried out.

The stage that ran from Fort Quitman along the San Antonio to El Paso line kept some of the troops busy escorting important people and regular citizens. At times this was not possible, and men died tragically and didn't finish their business. Such was the case with Maj. Gen. James J. Byrne, an employee of the Texas Pacific Railway. Major General Byrne stopped over in Fort Quitman on a team change and was soon on his way again. Checking the route for possible use by the railroad, Byrne studied the terrain alone in the coach when he noticed a cloud of dust rolling across the vast expanse of desert. Using his spyglass, he saw that the riders causing the dust were Mescaleros from Victorio's band of warriors. Getting his pistol ready, he stuck his head out to shout orders to the officer leading the troops and took a bullet in the chest. He died several hours later. Byrne's spirit has been seen roaming the area on unfinished railroad business.

Fort Quitman was evacuated on April 5, 1861, until after the Civil War. On January 1, 1868, Capt. Henry Carroll and Company F of the Ninth US Cavalry and the Twenty-fifth US Infantry reoccupied Fort Quitman, but it was not until February 25 that the reoccupation became official.

The fort was permanently abandoned in the spring of 1881, after the death of the Mescalero chief Victorio. A second post office operated four miles south of the ruins of the fort from 1926 until either 1937 or the late 1940s. In 1940, the residents of Fort Quitman numbered fewer than twenty-five, and by the mid-1950s the town was no longer shown on maps of the area. Fort Quitman is located twenty miles southeast of McNary, Texas, in southern Hudspeth County. Nothing remains of the old fort except a cemetery.

FORT GATES

The citizens in the vicinity of old Fort Gates usually ignore echoes from Lead Mountain, although there is one that cannot be ignored: It is the echo of a violinist's music. It is a most memorable sound for those lucky enough to hear it.

In 1849, Fort Gates was a sizable military facility compared to others established around the same time. Over the years, the number of enlisted men grew from 94 to 256, and the men's backgrounds varied widely.

One soldier, in particular, is remembered for the music he coaxed from his violin. Each evening around six o'clock, he would climb to the top of the hill overlooking the fort. Soon the beautiful music drifted down to the encampment, and most of the activity would cease while the soldiers stopped to listen to the same haunting refrain every night.

He poured his heart into his music. His violin told of his longing for home, where he'd left under a dark cloud and could never return. It told of remorse for the man he'd killed in self-defense and tears for the love he'd lost forever.

He had left New York, chosen the name Chandler, and joined the army to serve out his self-inflicted sentence of solitude. One night after he'd finished playing for the men, he and a friend began talking.

"When you kill a man over a woman, it hardly makes a difference if it was in self-defense or not."

"What are you saying, Chandler? Did you kill somebody?" Ducking his head, Chandler nodded.

"Over a woman?"

Again, Chandler nodded. "Yeah, she was my girl and I told him so. He wouldn't let go of her, and I grabbed his arm and tossed him to the ground."

"What happened, then?"

"When he stood up he had a knife in his hand. We fought and I pushed him away real hard. He fell on his own knife and it killed him. I got blamed for murdering him, and my girl hates me now. Before anyone could put me in jail, I left and came to Texas, joining the army under my mother's maiden name." Chandler rubbed his eyes to keep the tears at bay. "You know, when I think about her, my heart really hurts. I feel like it's going to kill me sometimes."

"Is that why you play the love song on your fiddle?"

"Well, yes, except it is a violin, not a fiddle. Katherine didn't like my music. She thought my playing made me less manly. From then on I never did play when I was in her presence. But I love to play. It makes me feel better."

"We don't think there's anything wrong with your playing. In fact, we like it. It gives us something to ease the tension from the day's work."

"Thanks, Charlie."

"You keep right on playing like you do. Nobody around here is going to tell you it isn't manly. I'll see to that for sure."

One night, while the last tender note died on the breeze, a Comanche brave stepped from behind a tree and raised his bow, aiming it at Chandler. The brave's arrow pierced Chandler's heart, and he fell to the ground. He was found the next morning still clutching his beloved violin.

Charlie commented it must be a sign, and the men decided Chandler should be buried on the hilltop. When the burial detail finished digging his grave, they laid the violin in his hands and lowered him into the earth.

Later the same evening around six o'clock, the haunting sounds of the love song drifted down from the hilltop, as if it had taken on the essence of the violin and the man. As the years have passed, the music from the hilltop has become faint, and only occasionally can it be heard.

Gen. George Mercer Brooke authorized one of the largest forts built on the Texas frontier. Fort Gates was originally established on October 26, 1849, as a stockade of eighteen buildings on the Leon River. Orders were revoked for a third company quarters after it was about half completed. Supplies were shipped in to Fort Gates via Washington-on-the-Brazos, Houston, and Indianola. Fort Gates troops were able to protect only the settlers in the fort's immediate radius of sixty to seventy miles.

Census rolls in 1850 listed six officers and ninety-four men at the fort. Troops included men from Company D, Company F,

Company H, and Company I, from which Chandler served, of the Eighth US Infantry. In April 1851, 256 enlisted men and 45 officers manned Fort Gates. This is reported to be the most men at the post in any single month.

Lying in the northern part of Tonkawa Indian country, Fort Gates frequently held off raids by the Waco, Comanche, and Lipan Apache Indians. The large number of troops stationed at Fort Gates helped in removing the menace of their attacks quickly. With this accomplished, the fort was no longer necessary and the army abandoned it in March 1852, one of the first forts to be closed. After a while the settlers dismantled the buildings for personal use, and only the rock fireplaces remain.

The mountain behind Fort Gates later became known as Lead Mountain because of the large number of lead bullets found during an archeological excavation. The site may have been used for a target range or the location of many bloody battles between troops and Indians. However, no records of any such battles were ever recorded.

Nothing except a historical marker is left of the formerly large outpost southeast of Gatesville 2.5 miles out on US Highway 36. Gatesville is in Coryell County, west of Waco, in an open field on private property.

FORT MASON

The residents in the valley below the headquarters building sleep through the nightly walks of one of Fort Mason's most famous commanders, Gen. Robert E. Lee.

In January and February of each year, the ghostly image of the famous general is often seen pacing the porch of the headquarters building. Most say Robert E. Lee is still contemplating his decision to leave the Texas frontier to go home to his family to help in the fight for the Confederacy. Robert E. Lee sometimes burns the midnight oil while sitting at a table inside the building. Several people have seen an oil lamp burning in the window when no one is supposed to be in the old fort building overlooking the beautiful valley below.

Robert E. Lee paced the porch, holding a letter. He paused to stare at his surroundings; the cold January air thick with moisture-laden clouds shrouded the rooftops of the houses in the valley.

He wondered how he could leave his post in Texas and yet, how could he not go home? His family and friends needed him. On the other hand, he had never shirked his duty to the army and this could be no different. He would have to wait and see if the Union did indeed dissolve. His decision had to be made soon. He would write a return letter to his son when he received word from Washington. His duties at Fort Mason would have to wait. After making his decision, Lee turned on his heel and entered the headquarters building.

On February 13, 1861, General Lee finally received his orders to report to the Chief of Staff in Washington, D.C., and left Fort Mason immediately for San Antonio.

The day wore on and nothing more was seen of Lee at Fort Mason's headquarters. Night crept into the sleepy valley below, and a gentle snow began to fall on the roofs. When the residents were snug in their beds and a veil of white blanketed the area, tiny lights from the windows sparkled in the darkness. Long into the night a lantern burned in the window of Fort Mason's headquarters.

My friend Sammy and I visited Fort Mason recently, and we were told of a mysterious figure that roamed the headquarters building. We decided to see for ourselves. Sure enough, as darkness covered the earth, a light from inside beamed forth, showing a shadowy figure in the window. Upon second glance we both agreed it appeared to be Robert E. Lee. Mesmerized by what we saw, we watched as Lee sat at the table, reading over a stack of papers in front of him.

He constantly rubbed his brow, concentrating on the pages. Picking up a quill, he dipped it into the inkwell and began writing. Dawn crept over the horizon and found Lee still at the table with his quill and ink handy. He reached for the lantern and turned

Robert E. Lee's ghost is said to haunt the porch of this headquarters building at Fort Mason.

down the flame, and then he stood, stretching his hands toward the ceiling. Robert E. Lee walked away from the window and faded into the shadows of the history of the Texas frontier.

Established on a hill in July 1851, Fort Mason sported twenty-three permanent buildings constructed for the troops. Only three short years later, in January 1854, troops abandoned Fort Mason, but Indian raids and depredations on the citizens in the vicinity made it necessary for Fort Mason to be reopened. Col. Albert Sidney Johnston and the Second Cavalry's 750 men traveled from Missouri to Fort Mason and reoccupied the fort. Used for regimental headquarters for six companies of troops in 1857, Fort Mason served the army well.

Another distinguished officer, Lt. John Bell Hood, and twenty-four of his soldiers left Fort Mason to fight a war party of nearly one hundred Comanches and Lipan Apache Indians. Only two of the twenty-four died in the skirmish, and five were wounded. The three-day patrol turned into a five-week siege.

A cannon stands guard at Fort Mason.

Tracking the Indians who led a raid on settlers in the Fort Mason district, Hood and his men lost the trail many times during the month they were on the hunt. When the detail finally caught up with the warriors, one of the Indians waved a white flag. Lieutenant Hood figured the Indians' flag for a trick, and sure enough, when he came out to meet them one-on-one, the twenty-four soldiers, including Hood, were sorely outnumbered. Although worn-out from the forced march, the soldiers fought gallantly. At the end of the cat-and-mouse chase, the Indians attacked in waves, surrounding the soldiers easily.

After a long, drawn-out battle, a full-blown, head-on attack by the Comanches ensued. This proved to be hand-to-hand combat in which only two soldiers were lost. The Indians retreated and set fire to the grass around the troops before scattering in every direction. Hood and his troops, including five wounded, made their way back to Fort Mason.

A restoration of Fort Mason began in 1975, spearheaded mainly by one individual in the area. Today, the fort belongs to the Mason County Historical Society.

There is one original building from the fort. It stands down the hill from the replica fort. It is recognized by its red stone and gun slits in the walls. It is on private property, but you can get a good look at it from the street.

Visitors can explore the reproduction officers' quarters at the Fort Mason Museum at 204 West Spruce Street in Mason, Texas.

FORT CHADBOURNE

Maggie Jackson's ghostly sobs are often heard on nights when a bright moon shines down on the narrow stream near the ruins of Fort Chadbourne. Her reflection can be seen in Oak Creek when the water is deep and clear. Beautiful auburn braids frame her pretty green eyes and heart-shaped face. Maggie still searches throughout the countryside for her murdered parents.

Fort Chadbourne, established in late autumn of 1852, saw only a few skirmishes with the unpredictable Comanches. In its sixteen years as a fortification, Fort Chadbourne boasted of many distinguished visitors, including Robert E. Lee, famed commanding officer of Confederate troops. The Butterfield Overland stage made stops at Fort Chadbourne before moving on westward.

In the spring of 1858, the Jackson family was to stop overnight at the safety of the small fort. Comanches lay in wait for the stage and attacked when it rumbled along the trail. The driver and the man riding shotgun were killed, leaving the people inside the stage unprotected from the Indians. David Jackson fired his pistol at the Comanches. His wife sat on the floor of the coach, protecting their daughter in her arms while the coach rocked and swayed. The two men in the opposite seats of the stage cowered next to each other, clinging to their cases.

"Do either of you have a gun?" David demanded.

"Of course, I have." One of the men pulled a pistol from his vest pocket but made no effort to use it.

Jackson fumed with anger. "Well, use the thing then! Shoot! They want to kill us, you fool."

The officers' quarters at Fort Chadbourne, on the Chadbourne Ranch near Bronte

The man stared at the small handgun and then, holding one hand over his ear, stuck the pistol out the window and pulled the trigger.

Jackson grabbed the pistol from the man and handed it to his wife.

"Here, Margaret. You can shoot better than he can."

A stray bullet hit the man's sample case. The bottles inside shattered, spilling elixir into his lap.

Comanche braves caught the bridles of the runaway team and halted the horses. Yanking open the stage doors, the Comanches dragged the men out of the coach. When they saw petite six-year-old Maggie and her mother, they became excited and pulled them out alongside the men. Maggie's beautiful red braids were coiled atop her head like her mother's, and the Comanches seemed fascinated with the color.

Frightened though she was, Margaret listened to the Indians' guttural language. One of the braves turned to the leader and pointed to Maggie. Margaret held her child close and guarded her against the Indians. The brave walked around them slowly and, taking a strand of Margaret's red hair in his hand, uttered a long spill of words to the others. Laughter erupted from the onlookers. Afraid of what she figured was to come, Margaret stiffened her back and pulled Maggie even closer.

When one of the braves jumped from his horse and grabbed Maggie, Margaret and David tried to stop him. The Comanche lanced David in the stomach and slashed Margaret's throat. The Comanche warriors disposed of the other passengers just as quickly. The small raiding party rode away with the horses and tiny Maggie, who sobbed from the horror of the murder of her parents and the others.

Upon reaching the campsite, the Comanche carried Maggie to his teepee, where his wife sat, still mourning the loss of her own child. He presented the weeping Maggie to his wife, the brave making note of the long red braids. The woman took Maggie in her arms and cuddled her close, softly humming to her.

Frightened, Maggie sobbed even more. In deep shock, the tiny girl whimpered for days. The warrior brought fresh meat for his

Maggie's Place occupies a corner devoted to the ghostly child that is said to reside among the ruins at Fort Chadbourne.

wife to prepare for the child; nevertheless, nothing the woman cooked tempted Maggie. Within days Maggie fell ill and soon died of starvation and a broken heart.

The brave and his wife took the child's tiny body to a stream near Fort Chadbourne where the stage had passed and laid her to rest on the bank. Shortly after the Comanches left the water's edge, a cavalry patrol from Fort Chadbourne rode past and discovered the child's body, the final victim of the massacre, but not before the stream assumed Maggie's sad spirit.

The soldiers took Maggie's body back to Fort Chadbourne for burial next to her parents, but her spirit roams the vicinity of where her parents were murdered.

During the Civil War Fort Chadbourne stood unmanned and abandoned. Then afterwards, when the troops returned, the fort boasted some three hundred soldiers. In the spring of 1868 the water supply played out, and the fort crumbled into ruins.

The Fort Chadbourne Foundation was established February 1, 1999, as a 501(c) 3 nonprofit charitable organization to preserve, stabilize, and partially restore the historic site of Fort Chadbourne and present it to the public. The fort site is open to the public for self-guided tours during daylight hours, seven days a week; there is no charge for touring the site, but donations are gladly accepted.

Since the inception of the foundation not only have all ruins been stabilized, but now several of the buildings have been restored, including the barracks, single officers' quarters, and cellar. The year 2017 marked the 150th anniversary of the Butterfield Overland stage, and the foundation hopes to break ground on the restoration of the Butterfield Overland Stage Stop at Fort Chadbourne. There is a temporary visitor center/museum that houses many artifacts found at the fort and it is located in the rock office, east of the fence line from the barrack buildings. This office is open from 8:00 a.m. to 5:00 p.m. during the week unless the staff is attending meetings, giving programs, etc. The fort also offers weekend and holiday appointments by contacting the foundation at (325)

743-2555 or (325) 473-5311. To visit Fort Chadbourne, take US Highway 277 out of Bronte northwest for about twelve miles. If you leave Robert Lee and drive east on US Highway 158, you will reach the Fort Chadbourne main gate; a huge spur will greet you at that gate. Perhaps you will see or hear Maggie when you arrive.

FORT MCKAVETT

A Boy Scout troop huddled around a campfire in front of Barracks Number Four at Fort McKavett, eating hot dogs and telling ghost stories. Each told their favorite story, trying to outdo the one previously told as a ghostly Buffalo Soldier eavesdropped on their party. The leaders smiled at one another and listened to the imaginings of the youngsters. As the hour grew late, one of the park rangers got up to add another log to the fire. He passed the barracks and peered up toward a window and stopped dead in his tracks. A Buffalo Soldier stood in the barracks, watching him from the window. Their gazes met and the soldier smiled, winked at the park ranger, and then saluted, slowly fading into the darkness of the empty barracks building. He was never seen again at the window by anyone else. He has, however, been heard from time to time, walking up and down some of the plank porches of Fort McKavett's buildings.

An administrative technician, fairly new to the Fort McKavett State Historical Park, had a chilling experience late one afternoon, near closing time. Hearing strange noises from the storage room across the hall from the gift shop, she looked around to see if anyone had entered. The wind was up, which was typical for West Texas, and since Fort McKavett was located at the top of a hill, she decided it must have been the storeroom door bumping against the doorjamb. She went to check on it and found the door was propped open as usual. Still apprehensive, she returned to her office in the gift shop. Soon her work was interrupted again, but this time by the sound of heavy footsteps pounding on the wooden porch.

"The footsteps were really heavy, like someone wearing work boots," she reported to the other rangers.

When she glanced out at the parking lot, she saw no vehicles other than her own, and she knew she was the only employee on duty that day.

"I just thought, well, it's nearly closing time, and one of the guys is playing a trick on me."

When she asked her coworkers about it the next day, she said they just smiled and told her that those boot sounds were more than likely the ghost of one of the Buffalo Soldiers who'd been seen around the fort from time to time. None of the employees at the fort was immune to a visit from the Buffalo Soldiers or others who dwelled at Fort McKavett.

Another incident involved one of the top rangers while he jogged around the park. He came upon what he thought was a man shouting orders to a group. The ranger supposed it was an Irishman, judging by the man's accent. He continued to jog his usual route, and the voices grew distant and then faded completely until he reached the north side of the parade grounds once more.

The park ranger began searching for the source of the voices, after he heard them several times, but found no one. He questioned his fellow rangers, describing the voices to them. The other workers assured him they had never heard the voices on the parade grounds calling troops to order.

"At the time I heard the man shouting, the park office didn't open to the public for another two hours," he stated. "Besides, none of the other employees would arrive for another hour or so.

"Apparently the main voice, the one doing the shouting, was very angry. It sounded as if he was reprimanding his men and in not too soft a voice, either. I heard another voice call him Sergeant."

The ranger has not heard the voices again, but he is not alone in seeing and hearing fort dwellers from the past. Many people who have visited the park have also experienced the special spirits who reside in many of the buildings of Fort McKavett.

The ruins of Fort McKavett show the rocks that can be found in the hills near Maynard.

The caretakers of this historical park are proud to have the ghostly guests around. They say it makes for some interesting times.

Fort McKavett was one of the posts on the Texas frontier that was built to last. This was due to a lack of Indian attacks in the area, causing the troops to be kept busy by using their labor for construction of the stone buildings. Fort McKavett was first established on March 14, 1852. It was originally called Camp San Sabá but later named for Capt. Henry McKavett, who had fallen in the battle of Monterey in 1846.

The area around Fort McKavett was quiet for such a long period of time that the army was ordered to abandon the encampment in February 1859, and the troops left in March. During the Civil War the buildings sheltered settlers and travelers.

At one point Fort McKavett rented out the officers' quarters to campers. Such was the case one weekend, when a couple visiting the park decided to stay. Just around dusk the lady was laying out supper when she heard a faint knock on the front door.

She figured it was the ranger who lived on the premises, and she opened the door. There in the wan light stood a little girl, smiling up at her. The woman thought the little girl might be the ranger's child who wandered away from her home or perhaps a child someone had left behind; she became worried. It wasn't until later that she realized the girl was dressed rather peculiarly, in a style more appropriate to the turn of the century.

"Will you come play with me?" the child innocently asked.

"Well, I don't know," the woman replied. "Where are your parents?"

The little girl shrugged and giggled as she turned to go. The girl began to run toward the ruins of the long barracks. The lady followed after, but before she could catch her, the girl disappeared behind a rock wall.

Between 1900 and 1910 a little girl's parents had stopped at Fort McKavett, seeking shelter for the night because their daughter was ill and there was a storm brewing. Before the sun came up the next morning, the girl had died, and the grieving parents buried their child before continuing on their westward journey.

Perhaps the child is looking for her parents or she's simply lonely and wants someone to play with her. She has appeared to more than one visitor at Fort McKavett.

My own experience at Fort McKavett was as dramatic. While touring the ruins and restored buildings, I got that tingly feeling of someone watching me from far away. My friend Sammy, who travels with me, had a bit of the feeling but not nearly as much as I seemed to. We walked past the old school, and then to the reconstructed officers' quarters. My goose bumps grew worse. As we peered inside, I felt as if I were intruding on someone's private life.

When we stopped at the headquarters building, the feeling hit me again. Someone or something didn't want us in this building. We stepped into the room, and it was rather cool for the time of day. I noticed there was a large safe sitting in front of the door. The safe door stood wide open. I looked carefully at the compartments and some of the papers inside it, commenting that it sure wasn't as large as one would expect. Walking on into the other room, I saw papers strewn on a table along one wall and a chalkboard in one corner. I noticed a sudden rise in temperature when we entered this room. It was quite a bit warmer than the front room and the remaining rooms in the building.

As we made the circle through the headquarters, we came back into the front room where the safe sat. Again this room was much cooler than the rest of the building. We turned to go and I noticed the safe door had been closed. I asked Sammy if she'd closed it. She said she had not, and the two of us were the only ones around who could have shut the door on the safe. It was apparent to me that someone didn't like me poking around inside the safe.

Shortly after we left the headquarters building, a guide drove up in his pickup and offered to take us inside the locked officers' quarters, where I felt like an intruder peering through the glass doors. We went inside the small cabin from the back door. The moment I stepped inside, that tingly feeling grabbed me and held on tight. Sammy told me she had the distinct feeling that someone had always placed geraniums on the windowsill of the front room, and it was at that point I began to smell the geraniums. I felt as if we were being watched as we strolled through the house.

Sammy and the park ranger went into the back of the home while I was still taking pictures in the middle section of the house. As I started to follow them, I looked up into a mirror hanging above the fireplace. Gazing back at me was the face of a young woman, smiling brightly. Her dark brown hair was in a neat bun on top of her head, and her high-collared shirtwaist was an off-white print with a brownish skirt. I turned to see if she was standing behind me, but no one was there. When I looked back at the mirror, I saw my own reflection. I asked the others if they'd seen her too, but neither of them had. The park ranger said that one time when he had come in to clean the house, he had found some very sophisticated drawings on the chalk slate on the table, and

one of the other guides erased it. Several days later another drawing was found on the slate. Unfortunately it was destroyed also,
and there have been no more drawings since that time.

In April 1868, when the troops returned after the war, the
officers' quarters were the only buildings at Fort McKavett that
were inhabitable. The Fourth Cavalry and the three companies
of black soldiers who were members of the 38th Infantry reconstructed the fort.

A small settlement called "Scabtown" grew up along the
opposite bank of the river. This little town caused many discipline
problems for the commanding officers because of its saloons and
bawdy houses. Most of the soldiers spent their earnings here.

When Col. Ranald S. Mackenzie took command of the troops
in 1869, he combined the Thirty-eighth and the Forty-first Infantry troops to form the Twenty-fourth Infantry of the US Army,
later known as the famed Buffalo Soldiers. The remaining troops
of the Buffalo Soldiers included the Twenty-fifth Infantry and the
Ninth and Tenth Cavalry.

Instead of doing much Indian fighting in the immediate area
of Fort McKavett, the troops helped to support other campaigns
in the neighboring districts. By the time the Indian wars were over
in Texas, the troops at Fort McKavett were closing down operations there. On June 30, 1883, the fort was no longer needed so the
army officially abandoned Fort McKavett, once called "the netti-
est post in Texas" by Gen. William T. Sherman.

With the Indian threat gone, the civilians of Fort McKavett stayed on; some occupied the Fort McKavett buildings and
others stayed outside the fort. By the mid-1890s the community
boasted about eighty people, a weekly newspaper, two hotels,
three churches, and a broom and mattress factory. In 1904, the
school enrolled twenty-eight students. By the 1920s, Fort McKavett's population numbered about 150, until the Great Depression. The numbers continued to fall and by 1990, the town was
called home by only forty-five people. Today, only a smattering of

ranchers live in the area, but, amazingly, the post office remains open.

Efforts to restore Fort McKavett began in the late 1960s, and today the Fort McKavett State Historical Park is one of the best preserved and most intact examples of a Texas Indian Wars military post.

Numerous buildings remain at the site, some have been rebuilt or restored, and others still lie in ruins. The old post hospital serves as the visitor center and museum. Several officers' quarters still stand, as well as the church, headquarters, morgue, and others. Other structures have crumbled, including some of the barracks and the bakery.

Nearby is the Fort McKavett Cemetery, which was established in 1849 and still used today. Most, but not all, of the soldiers buried at the cemetery were moved to other military cemeteries when the fort closed, but two interesting graves remain. They are the graves of William McDougall, who was killed in an Indian raid on the post on August 6, 1866, and John W. Vaden, who was shot in cold blood by the gunfighter Ben Daniels on October 7, 1886.

Fort McKavett is located at the intersection of Farm Roads 864 and 1674, twenty miles southwest of Menard, Texas.

FORT MARTIN SCOTT

Fort Martin Scott was first established on December 5, 1848, and was called Camp Houston. When Capt. Seth Eastman arrived with troops from Companies D and H of the First US Infantry, they opened one of the first US Army posts on Texas's western frontier. Eastman remained at Fort Martin Scott for only a few months until his orders came through to establish Fort Inge near present-day Fredericksburg.

The influx of settlers into the Pedernales Valley caused friction between the already friendly Germans and the Comanches. Some of the new settlers in the area didn't like the trade policy the Germans had with the Indians. They wanted some of the trade but were not willing to pay the same prices for the Indians' furs and other items. The settlers attempted to force the Indians to trade with them, and, being a bit hostile to the settlers anyway, the Comanches gathered several other tribes together to attack the settlers. Alarmed, Indian agent John R. Rollins and Capt. Hamilton Merrill arranged a meeting with the leaders of the tribes in an effort to prevent the hostilities.

Captain Merrill agreed to use his troops to escort the settlers and their representatives on the peacemaking expedition. He led his troops to the meeting on the San Sabá River at a slow, steady pace. With no way of knowing how the threatening situation would turn out, he kept a careful watch around the countryside. One never knew what to expect when dealing with the Comanches.

The Germans rode to the meeting site in wagons in front of the column of troops, sure of the dealings they'd had in the past with the Indians, thinking everything would be well.

Wishing to speak with Mr. Rollins once more, Capt. Merrill sent for the Indian agent.

"What did you want with me, Captain?"

"Explain to me again what the Indians want and what the settlers want," he said. "I'm not familiar with the situation, since I've only been at this post a short time."

"Well, sir, the Indians were accustomed to trading with the Germans, who have been working with them for years. The new settlers came in and have tried to take the Indian trade away from the Germans, but the Indians don't want them here. They want the settlers to leave them alone and go away." Rollins took a deep breath and waited for Captain Merrill's answer.

"I still don't understand." Captain Merrill recalled what he had read in the report. "According to the settlers, they have tried to deal fairly with the Indians in their trading."

"Yes, sir, that is what I have been told, but the Indians say the settlers, not the Germans, have sold them spoiled meat, bug-ridden

Fort Martin Scott in Fredericksburg has been reconstructed next to the Ranger Station.

grains, and other defective merchandise. They also claim the settlers charge exorbitant prices for these goods and won't pay fair for their furs. Sir, the Germans have been dealing with the Indians for years out here, and I think they should be allowed to continue. If the other settlers want to deal with the Indians, let them meet the quality and the prices of the Germans." The two men rode along in silence the remainder of the trip.

John Rollins had taken the commission of Indian agent at the request of a friend in Washington. He didn't like the Indians any better than most white men; nevertheless, someone had to keep the peace. He would speak for the Indians because his job prescribed it and he was a fair-minded man. While the company of troops neared the river, they saw a number of settlers standing off to one side, watching suspiciously while the handshakes went around in the groups of Comanches and Germans.

Captain Merrill stepped under the awning of the meeting tent, and everyone turned to listen when he cleared his throat.

"You men gather around here and let's get this started."

One of the outbuildings at Fort Martin Scott

The German spokesman stepped forward and took a seat at the table. One by one each representative of the parties concerned sat at the table. For hours they argued back and forth until each of the details of an agreement was hashed out to the satisfaction of everyone involved. The Fort Martin Scott Treaty, as it became known, agreed to end the fighting between the Germans, the Indians, and the other settlers. It prevented an impending full-blown war between the Comanche, the Wichitas, the Lipan Apaches, and the white settlers.

Settlers pushed farther west, and Fort Martin Scott lost its usefulness and became a forage depot for some time. In December 1853 the threat of the Indians against the settlers had mostly disappeared, and the army abandoned the fort.

Briefly, however, in September 1866, a detachment from the Fourth US Cavalry arrived to man the fort, and they stayed until that December, when the army formally closed Fort Martin Scott.

Local citizens claim they have seen the long-ago peacemakers on the hill overlooking the Fort Martin Scott site, sitting around a long table, hashing out some disagreement. When the arguments were over, the peaceful ghosts faded into nothingness to argue another day.

Visitors to Fredericksburg can celebrate Texas at Fort Martin Scott Days, experiencing when the fort was an active military post and headquarters for the Gillespie County Mounted Volunteers and Texas State Troops from 1847 to 1866. The events place much emphasis on the military history, and include that with civilian living history to the time period. Generally Friday is School Day and Saturday is general admission.

Fort Martin Scott events are organized and operated by Fort Martin Scott Friends. They ask reenactors to join them from Thursday evening through Saturday afternoon. They have a welcoming reception on Thursday. On Friday and Saturday they serve breakfast goods, box lunches, and campfire suppers, featuring music and storytelling.

To reach the park, drive three miles southeast of Fredericksburg on State Highway 290 and you will see the historical marker.

FORT PHANTOM HILL

From the time the soldiers arrived at Fort Phantom, some of them heard whispered words of love on the breezes. November 14, 1851, dawned no different from any other day on Phantom Hill, except for the five companies of the Fifth Infantry who came to establish the post on the Clear Fork of the Brazos River.

Upon arrival to Fort Phantom Hill, Lieutenant Colonel Abercrombie halted his troops, giving orders to make camp. Winter winds assaulted the hillside, a blowing force through the blackjack oak trees and prickly pears.

Sentries were posted around the camp perimeter while the remaining soldiers bedded down for the night. The howling winds shook the tents of the men as the sentries huddled in their inadequate woolen coats waiting for the dawn. Clouds rolled in from the north, scudding across the sky, making shadows on the moon.

Late in the evening after the first sentry change, a couple of the troopers met at the western edge of the cliff that dropped off into the valley. Checking to make sure there were no signs of Indians, they started back toward the tents. A strong gust of cold wind blew across their path, and suddenly a cloud of misty smoke formed before them.

"What is that?"

The soldier stared in horror as his partner stammered an answer, "It's a ghost!"

A mystical figure appeared and floated nearer. Both men scrambled to escape, diving to the ground when a puff of extremely cold smoke passed overhead. They leapt to their feet and tried to run, but they were unable to move.

An Indian wrapped in a wispy white buffalo robe stood several feet from the soldiers. They watched, mesmerized, as he opened his wrap and a woman stepped from the circle of his arms, laughing. The laughter died in the howl of the wind, and she disappeared. Chilled to the bone, the soldiers gazed at the Indian. His retreat was swift and silent, leaving no trace of his ever being at Fort Phantom Hill.

The next morning, the soldiers told their story to their buddies and were laughed at and shunned. When they reported what they saw to their commanding officer, they were put in the guardhouse for drinking on duty.

More than once the ghostly lovers have appeared, and, according to the stories passed down from one generation to the next, the spirits changed from two to one, and on other occasions even different apparitions have appeared.

If you are visiting Fort Phantom Hill, the spirits will be there—maybe not visibly, but in the wind that blows across the plains and through the ghostly chimneys still standing. Listen closely and you will hear the clanking of harness hardware and the *chink chink* of spurs echoing from the valley below and the echo of a sergeant calling his troops to attention.

The chimneys at Fort Phantom stand guard like sentinels of the past.

Aromas rise from the small bakery building, and the sound of a stonemason's hammer rings out as he works on the buildings. If not for cactus growing on top of abandoned chimneys haunting the skyline, smoke might be seen curling silently upward, as if to reach up and wrap the ghostly lovers in a warm embrace.

Fort Phantom Hill, formerly known as "Post on the Clear Fork of the Brazos," was, like all other Texas forts, built to aid and protect the settlers and the men and women traveling to the goldfields of California.

As isolated as it was, making it vulnerable to Indian attack, Fort Phantom Hill actually had a friendly relationship with the Indians in the vicinity, including the Penateka Comanches led by Buffalo Hump. Other tribes who visited the fort were groups of Lipans, Wichitas, Kiowas, and Kikapoos. At one time even a party of Delaware Indians held a ceremony at Fort Phantom Hill while preparing for a buffalo hunt.

The army at Fort Phantom Hill had even employed Indian scouts. Jim Shaw and Black Beaver were among the better-known

The ruins of a burned-out officers' quarters at Fort Phantom hold many mysteries.

scouts used at the fort from the Delaware tribe. Eventually, though, Fort Phantom Hill lost its usefulness.

The first abandonment of Fort Phantom Hill came on the heels of a command change on April 6, 1854. As the garrison marched out of sight of the compound, smoke swirled to the sky until all the wooden structures of the fort were engulfed in flames. Some say an army wife hated the fort so much that she started the fire. Others cite Union sympathizers, while still others say the Indians were the guilty party. More inconclusive than not, though, the majority of the evidence points to a couple of disgruntled soldiers who swore that no one would ever have to set foot on the hill again.

One man tells of when he was a child playing at the ruins of Fort Phantom Hill. He was a rock collector and had lived nearby. Every day after getting his chores done, Alan would walk to where the fort once stood, and, as kids often do, he played cowboys and Indians. He stepped inside the square of stones that at one time were an officers' quarters.

"It seemed like the walls just built up around me magic like. I was standing there in a really cold room."

At first he was frightened but then he decided to look around. To his further amazement, he heard voices behind him, and two men came through the door. Their conversation was low and garbled, but he did hear the word "fire" distinctly. As the two men passed by him and walked to a table in the center of the room, they bent over the table and started whispering more.

Alan watched them for quite some time until he heard his mother calling him, at which time the men and the walls of the officers' quarters faded.

In 1858 the stone buildings were repaired, and the fort was used as a way station by the Southern Overland Mail. It was used sporadically by other groups such as buffalo hunters, more troops on temporary orders, and a company of Mackenzie's Raiders. A small town grew up in the area with a small population. One of the last reports commented that there was nothing but one hotel, one saloon, a general store, a blacksmith shop, and ten thousand prairie dogs.

Fort Phantom Hill was on private property, but the primary thirty-eight-acre site where Fort Phantom Hill stood was given to the Fort Phantom Foundation in 1997 by Mr. and Mrs. Jim Alexander of Abilene, Texas. The site has been open to the public since 1972 and is now completely maintained and operated by the foundation. The public is welcome to visit the three original stone buildings that are left, as well as several chimneys still standing watch over the old fort site.

The Fort Phantom Foundation is a nonprofit organization supported by grants and donations from individuals and organizations. Fort Phantom Hill is open to visitors daily from dawn until dusk. Landmarks are labeled with signs, and the site is open for self-guided tours, free of charge. There is ample parking space, and, surprisingly, this rustic site offers nice public restroom facilities in the new visitor center, where you can find free brochures of the area.

Take Interstate 20 out of Abilene to the east and exit onto FM 600. Drive about fourteen miles to Fort Phantom Hill in Jones County. The physical address is 10818 FM 600, Abilene, Texas.

FORT RINGGOLD

Late at night when all is quiet, screams of terror and agony can be heard near where a large oak tree once stood. A body can be seen swinging by the neck in the night breeze, and then it will vanish in the blink of an eye. Shortly afterward, the chatter of Gatling gun fire echoes through the midnight sky.

Fort Ringgold is one of the best preserved of Texas's frontier forts and one of the oldest, with ninety-six years of service to the US Army.

Fort Ringgold was established on October 26, 1848, at the end of the Mexican War, to stand guard over the border and Rio Grande City. Fort Ringgold held the honor of being the post farther south than any other on the western frontier of Texas. Bvt. Maj. Joseph H. LaMotte and two companies of the First US Infantry stopped at the Davis Landing, where the army had leased lands for the building of the fort.

Several interruptions marred the fort's many years of service. Its major periods of service were from 1848 until 1861, when it was abandoned because of the Civil War. It was re-garrisoned in 1865, and troops occupied it until the Philippines Crisis in 1906, at which time troops were pulled out of Fort Ringgold once more. Again in 1917 troops filled the barracks and were there until 1944, when it was sold as surplus property.

In the nineteenth century Fort Ringgold saw such prominent people in its compound as Robert E. Lee, John J. Pershing, and even Jefferson Davis. The post held the area's first telegraph office, fueled the local economy, and protected the area from smugglers, rustlers, and insurrectionists. Ringgold troops were involved in ending the Cortina War during the Mexican Revolution under the command of Maj. Samuel P. Heintzelman when he joined forces with John Salmon Ford and the Texas Rangers in 1860.

One of the worst times for Fort Ringgold was in 1899 when Troop D of the Ninth US Cavalry was garrisoned at the fort after returning triumphantly from the Cuban campaign. Racial tensions between the citizens of Rio Grande City and the troops were at an all-time high amid conflicting reports of impending attacks on the fort and the town.

One evening just before sunset, two of the black soldiers stationed at Fort Ringgold stood at their post. George was to go and visit his parents, but they lived in servants' quarters where they worked on the white side of town.

"You can't go over there no more, George. Them people are mean, and they don't want us black men over there in their neighborhood."

"I know what you're saying is the truth, Joseph, but I have to go. The folks my parents work for are there across the tracks and I gotta see my mama and papa. I haven't seen them in three years since I joined up with this outfit. They don't know if I'm dead or alive."

"George, you go over there and you'll get dead for sure. Then what about your parents?"

George shrugged. "If that's the way it has to be, then it will be. Either way, I am going to see my folks."

Joseph watched his buddy of several years and battles dress in his best uniform and leave the fort with his signed pass. Somehow knowing that he would never see his friend alive again, Joseph ran after him and hugged George tightly.

"What's that all about? You want somebody to see us hugging like that?"

"Just in case, George. Just in case." Joseph turned and ran back to the barracks.

George shook his head. That boy could be strange sometimes.

He was a good friend, though, and he always meant well. They'd seen many battles together, especially in the Cuban campaign. He and Joseph had both received commendations for their fighting over there. Touching the medal hanging from his uniform, he could still see the look on Joseph's face when the commander had pinned it. Yep, his mama would be proud of that medal, too. He could hardly wait to surprise her when he showed up at their door.

He'd gotten directions from one of the men at the fort who'd been in Rio Grande City many times. As luck would have it though, the Wilsons were rich white folks and lived right in the middle of the biggest white neighborhood in town. Yes, it was dangerous for him to be there at night, but he couldn't have made it any sooner. The Sarge wouldn't let him off during the day, so he just had to chance it at night. Reaching the Wilson's house was the easy part. Coming back to the fort late in the evening would be the riskiest part of the trip.

When he started to leave his parents' home behind the Wilson's big old house, George was running late. He hated to be late. The sergeant could really yell at a body and that was embarrassing. "Is there a shortcut back to the fort, Papa?"

"Yes, Son, but it's too rough for you to be going through at night."

"I'll be all right. Just map out the way for me, please. I don't want to be late."

His father told him about the shortcut, and he kissed his mama goodbye and hugged his father. Taking off at a run, George headed back.

Several blocks from the fort where he'd be home free, George ran into a crowd of drunken men on their way out of a seedy bar. One of the men grabbed George's arm, propelling him to the ground.

"Where do you think you're going in such an all-fired hurry, boy?"

"Back to Fort Ringgold." Sullenly, George climbed to his feet. Dusting off his uniform, he started on his way.

Grabbing his arm again, the man stopped George once more.

"Whoa, there. We didn't tell you to leave yet. What are you running so fast for? Did you try to steal something and get caught?"

"No, sir. I am going to be late for bed check at the barracks. I got to go." George tried to leave.

Another man caught George's arm and spun him around. "We didn't say you could go anywhere. Did we, boys?"

The men nodded, laughing darkly.

"Nope, sure didn't. I think this boy needs a lesson in manners so he knows how to act next time he sees us." The man winked at his buddies.

Before George knew what was happening, the white men had placed a rope around his neck and were leading him to the big oak tree out in front of Fort Ringgold.

"Don't look at us like that. We're just gonna teach you not to be late no more. Your sergeant will be proud of us for this lesson you're gonna learn."

George felt the rope tighten on his neck as the men threw it across the tree limb. He knew it was best not to fight them, and he whispered a prayer that they'd get tired of their game before long so he wouldn't be late. If he were, at least maybe the Sarge wouldn't be too mad when he gave his excuse.

Something happened moments later that made George's whispered prayer his last words. The man pulled the rope tighter, bringing George up to his tiptoes to keep from choking. Suddenly one of the men, who was much heavier than George, got his feet tangled in the rope and fell backwards, pulling George off the ground and strangling him to death.

The men were so drunk they didn't realize what was happening to George. When the man was freed of the rope, George's body slumped to the ground lifeless. The man's friends slapped each other on the back, laughing more. They left the scene, not checking to see if George was alive or dead.

The next morning George's body was found under the old oak tree. The rope was still around his neck, and his hands were tied behind his back with his own tie. As a member of Troop D of the Ninth US Cavalry who fought in the Cuban campaign, he was buried with full military honors.

This incident heightened the tensions between the troops at the fort and the townspeople. No one knew who the men were who had hanged the soldier, and if they did, they weren't talking. Rumors flew that the townspeople were going to attack Fort Ringgold. Before this could actually happen, 2nd Lt. E. H. Rubottom ordered a Gatling gun to be fired on an area between the fort and town. A few minor injuries occurred, but the supposed attacked was quelled before it ever got started. Of course, an investigation ensued but failed to show any specifics. No one was arrested and no charges were brought against Rubottom for acting unwisely.

After the inquisition into the hanging of the trooper, Governor Joseph Sayers sided with the Rio Grande citizens in asking the Ninth Cavalry to be removed from Fort Ringgold. It was requested that a garrison entirely made up of white Americans be maintained at the fort.

In 1947, the remains of troopers from the Fort Ringgold cemetery were taken to Fort Sam Houston in San Antonio, where they were interred at the National Cemetery.

The Rio Grande Consolidated Independent School District purchased the fort property in 1949. Since 1988 the district has maintained the standing buildings, the best known of which is the Lee House, where Robert E. Lee resided in 1860. The fort was placed on the National Register of Historic Places in 1993.

You can see what remains of Fort Ringgold by taking a tour of the Rio Grande City School grounds, one-quarter mile southeast of the junction of US Highway 83 and State Highway 755, in Rio Grande City.

CAMP COOPER

At Camp Cooper, Kiowa Joe, a half-Kiowa Indian, worked as a scout for the army. Shortly after the fort was established in early 1856, Joe appeared from out of nowhere. He rode in on his bony horse and stopped at the headquarters building. Joe stepped up on the porch of the log building and strolled inside.

"I want to talk to Lt. Col. Robert E. Lee."

The aide stared at him.

"The colonel is busy right now and he told me not to disturb him for anything, so you'll have to wait."

"I have information he's going to want to hear, so you'd better tell him I'm here."

The corporal looked doubtful. "Just who are you?"

"Most call me Kiowa Joe."

"All right." The young officer wrote the name on a slip of paper and slid it in between some papers on his desk.

"Aren't you going to tell Lee I am out here?"

"I have my orders, and I won't disturb the colonel for someone with no last name."

Joe quickly stepped behind the corporal's desk and held a knife to the officer's throat. "Now, you listen to me, you young whelp. I want to talk to Lee right now, and I am not opposed to going over your head or lack of one to do it. Do I make myself clear?"

The corporal carefully nodded.

"Now stand up real slow and go knock on that door or you won't be needing any lunch today or any other day."

The corporal knocked. "What is it, James?"

"There's someone to see you, sir."

"I thought I told you I didn't want to be disturbed."

"Well, yes, sir, you did, but Colonel, sir, he's holding a knife to my throat."

The door burst open and Lee stepped into the room. "What the devil is the meaning of this?"

"I'm Kiowa Joe. He didn't tell ya that, and I got an Indian report. I know who it was that escaped the reservation and I know where they are."

"Let go of that man and I'll talk to you."

Kiowa Joe put his knife away and stepped back from the corporal. "See? I told you he'd talk to me." Grinning broadly at Lee and the corporal, Joe entered Lee's office.

For the nineteen months that Robert E. Lee commanded the troops at Camp Cooper, Kiowa Joe scouted for the soon-to-be-famous commander.

Later, in October 1859, two years after Lee left Camp Cooper, it has been said that Kiowa Joe provided important information for the Cimarron Expedition that left from Camp Cooper, but there are no written records of that happening.

Men like Kiowa Joe who gathered information were essential to the army. I believe one of these men, if not Kiowa Joe, knew all along where Cynthia Ann Parker was for the twenty-four years she lived with the Comanches. Possibly such a person was responsible for the rangers knowing where and when to attack the village of Chief Nocona's people that led to the rescue of Cynthia Ann. After her recovery, the rangers brought Cynthia Ann back to Camp Cooper, where one of her uncles, Isaac Parker, came to find his niece in January 1861.

Only a few weeks later, on February 21, 1861, Camp Cooper was abandoned by the army, leaving the settlers of the Throckmorton area to fend for themselves against the Indians left in the area.

The Civil War and the reconstruction period that followed did little to keep the threat of Indian attacks down in Throckmorton County. In 1864 a war party near Elm Creek descended on a ranch and massacred twelve people and took six women and children captive. A short three years later, Indians murdered three youths near where Camp Cooper once stood.

A few days after the youths were murdered, Kiowa Joe was seen drunk and crawling around on the floor of a nearby saloon, looking for the price of another drink. A couple of rowdies collared him and roughed him up before they tossed him out into the night. Kiowa Joe was never seen alive again.

On occasion Kiowa Joe has been seen riding his bony old horse through the thickets that surround the Camp Cooper area. There has never been an explanation to this day for his disappearance or why he still tracks through the nearby meadow.

In 1906, J. B. Putnam purchased the property where Camp Cooper had been located from J. A. Matthews. The property is still in the Putnam family today. Camp Cooper is located in Throckmorton County, ten miles South of Throckmorton, Texas, on US Highway 283. At the junction of County Road 2584, turn west and drive for a few miles to County Road 2528, and then turn left and drive a few more miles. This is private property, so you must make an appointment to visit the site. Call (325) 762-2945.

FORT ESPERANZA

Seagulls wheel and screech their calls of caution along the beach. Sea waves crash into the ruins of what was Fort Esperanza. Another sound can be heard if you listen closely—the voice of a woman screaming in tortured pain competes with the gulls for attention. Looking for the body that belongs to the voice is futile. The crying woman died serving the Confederacy in 1863. Only when the tide is coming in can she be heard, begging for mercy from the butchers who tortured her for more information. Fort Esperanza, an earthen-work fortress, was constructed to protect Matagorda Bay from possible Union invasion into Texas in December 1861. Because the prior fort, built in 1842–1843, had more exposure than Confederate colonel R. R. Garland liked, he thought it best to reposition it about halfway up the island's front beach.

In February 1862, more additions to Fort Esperanza were made. The Confederates believed ships larger than gunboats could not get through the shallow water pass, and they were right in that one aspect. It did not, however, stop the Union from forcing their way through to the bay and capturing Galveston in September 1862.

The Union troops passed Fort Esperanza on October 25, 1862, in favor of attacking a weaker position, and the Confederates had to retreat to Indianola to defend the port. When the Union soldiers arrived to find the rebel soldiers were resisting at Port Lavaca, they were forced to withdraw from Matagorda Bay.

This left no ground forces at Fort Esperanza, and the Union army forfeited the garrison back to the Confederate soldiers.

Miss Lissett Hamilton did her part to help alert the Confederates to the plans of the Union soldiers until her activities were discovered. Despite pleas to the contrary, Union soldiers took Miss Hamilton prisoner and told her that if she did not reveal her source and her contacts on both sides, she would suffer the consequences.

A proud young woman and sure she would not come to any harm, Miss Hamilton refused to admit to any of the accusations against her good name. The Union officer in charge of breaking her story turned her over to several of his cruelest men and told them he wanted to know everything from her at any cost. The soldiers took Miss Hamilton to the lowest section of the fort walls at the seaside shore and began their interrogation.

For two days, Miss Hamilton endured the torture the soldiers dealt her and never revealed the information they wanted. When the third day dawned, the soldiers had stripped her of her clothing and staked her to the wall on the east side of Fort Esperanza where the tide would be corning in. While the day wore on, Miss Hamilton found herself being slowly covered with water. Only when the waves became harder and crashed against her body did she begin to beg for release. The waves crashed into her again and again, filling the depression where she stood until she drowned. She took her information with her to a watery grave.

Fort Esperanza changed hands from the Confederacy to the Union and back to the Confederacy until June 15, 1864. The Confederate soldiers took control one last time and held the fort until the end of the Civil War, at which time the army abandoned Fort Esperanza.

The fort's remaining turf-covered walls have eroded and drifted out to sea with the tides. The shoreline has increased and some of the outlying emplacements and rifle pits can no longer be traced along the beach. The old fort grounds are part of the

Matagorda Island National Wildlife Refuge. The topography of the area changes with each major hurricane that strikes, so currently the site of Fort Esperanza is under water. The location of the fort on the eastern shore of Matagorda Island cannot be accurately pinpointed because of all the changes due to the weather.

FORT GRAHAM

Out near Lake Whitney, tourists have seen the ghost of Apache Dan, a half-Indian army scout. Dan searches for his old stomping grounds where he bought whiskey and guns from the trading post owned by George Barnard.

Dan, who was wrongly accused, has faded into the pages of history and is heard from or seen only in our dreams.

Maj. Ripley Allen Arnold occupied Fort Graham in March 1849, along with Bvt. Brig. Gen. William S. Harney, and was accompanied by Company F and Company I of the Second US Dragoons. General Harney commanded the entire frontier district of Texas. National Archives show Fort Graham was named for James D. Graham; however, other sources say it was named in honor of Lt. Col. William M. Graham of the Second Dragoons. James Graham was with the Corps of Topographical Engineers.

Like many other forts established at the same time, Fort Graham became the northern anchor for the line of frontier defenses between the Towash Indian village and Fort Wichita in Indian Territory now known as Oklahoma. Major Arnold had orders to do several things with the establishment of Fort Graham. He and his troops were to provide escorts for supply trains and travelers. They were to patrol up to the forks of the Trinity River, protecting the settlers from Indian attacks, and were instructed to try to establish friendly terms with the Indians in the immediate area.

Major Arnold arrived at the Fort Graham site with eighty-nine men and officers to begin building the fort. During the first month, the troops managed to put together a number of clapboard and log buildings. Patrol duty, however, took the soldiers away from construction labors, and civilians were hired to build the remaining necessary structures.

A report filed by Major Arnold in April showed that out of the eighty-nine men who started with him the month before, only fifty-five men remained on his roster. This number included five officers and seven noncommissioned officers. The reason for this loss of manpower did not show up in the paperwork. When Major Arnold received orders to open yet another fort, he took Company F of the Second Dragoons with him, leaving Fort Graham with only one officer and forty-six men under the command of Lt. Fowler Hamilton.

Fort Graham eventually became a "listening post" for the northeast section of Texas. The Indian agents used Fort Graham for its headquarters during their visits to the Indian villages and nearby camps. George Barnard located his trading post near Fort Graham. The rumor of the charges that George Barnard sold guns and liquor to the Indians could never be proved, although the Indian agents tried many times to do so.

Apache Dan frequented this trading post and soon hired on with the army to report activities at the trading post. Apache Dan, being half-Indian, could pose for a full blood and no one would be the wiser. When he came to Fort Graham, Dan only wanted a handout, but Lt. W. H. C. Whiting told him he would have to work for what he wanted.

After Lieutenant Whiting explained why he needed someone to act as the army's eyes and ears at Barnard's trading post, Apache Dan agreed. He and Barnard did not get along well, and Dan had a vendetta against Barnard. He would like nothing better than to see the fat man out of business.

For many months, Dan stayed around Barnard's post, scrounging for coins dropped here and there by those who came to drink and purchase goods. The patrons called Dan a drunk, a no-good half-breed, and various other derogatory names. Apache Dan, however, knew each of the traders on a first-name basis and reported back to Whiting who bought what and when.

A new commander, Major Sibley, soon replaced Whiting. He didn't like Dan and told him his services were no longer needed. Apache Dan talked to the post surgeon at Fort Graham, and Josephus M. Steiner began taking Dan's reports. When Dan became frightened to tell what he'd seen and heard, Steiner upped the ante and Dan talked. He told of a major whom he'd heard making a deal to sell army horses to certain people for a huge profit. The Indians were ending up with the horses, which meant probable attack.

With further information revealed by Apache Dan, Steiner had every bit of evidence he needed to confront Maj. Ripley Arnold. Of course, Major Arnold denied the allegations. He even told a friend of his, "I will put him out of the way; he shall not give evidence against me." In a confrontation between the two, Josephus Steiner shot and killed Major Arnold. Apache Dan witnessed the gunplay and tried to leave but was killed in the process by a soldier who thought the Indian had murdered the commanding officer. Steiner later proved his theory about Arnold with the help of his attorney, the future governor Richard Coke.

Fort Graham troops continued to escort the travelers and mail coaches, and they kept their status as a listening post through 1852. By 1853 the settlers had pushed far enough west to render Fort Graham no longer strategically economical.

Fort Graham permanently closed on November 9, 1853. Although no major battles occurred in or around the fort, its Indian agent affairs made it one of the most important to the northeast Texas area.

In 1936, the Texas Centennial Commission purchased the land where Fort Graham stood. After purchasing the land, no reconstruction was ever done, and in 1970 the construction of Lake Whitney began. The only remaining building, a rock barracks, had been restored as part of the Texas Centennial celebration in 1936. But after the Brazos was dammed to create Lake Whitney, the building frequently flooded. It was torn down and moved, stone by stone, to higher ground in the 1980s, just a short distance east of its original location.

A group of archeology and anthropology students from Southern Methodist University excavated a portion of the old fort site in the early 1970s. Among the items they found were pieces of lamps, buttons, and stone points. These points were used on atlatls, spear-like weapons that the Indians hurled like a slingshot. Little remains now of the once formidable fort that helped to protect early Hill County settlers.

To visit Lake Whitney and perhaps get a glimpse of Apache Dan's spirit roaming around the lake area, drive out of Hillsboro, Texas, on State Highway 22 about twenty miles.

FORT CROGHAN

Travelers have often seen Sarah Ann Morgan driving her wagon through a misty haze when she nears the area close to where Fort Croghan once stood. A baby's cry is heard while Sarah tries to calm the child and drive the team of horses at the same time. When the team and wagon slip through the cloudiness shrouding the ground, the wagon careens around a slight curve in the road and crashes into the water.

On the windy afternoon of March 13, 1849, Henry McCulloch and his rangers rode up onto the east bank of Hamilton Creek and decided a fort should be built there to protect the settlers from Indian attacks. Five days later, the site became officially and militarily established under the command of Lt. C. H. Tyler and his troops.

This particular site lasted only a few months. On October 12, 1849, the temporary campsite for Fort Croghan moved another three miles farther up Hamilton Creek to a shallower crossing. Fort Croghan served under several names.

Fort Croghan's buildings were constructed by the troops, who used mostly oak posts covered with shingles. A few of the structures were made of logs. These houses served as officers' quarters.

By 1852 the Second Dragoons of the US Cavalry were headquartered at Fort Croghan. When December 1852 rolled around, most of the troops were stationed at one or more of the forts farther west on the frontier, and by 1853 the troops were deployed to other posts.

Indians in the area remained a harassing threat to the settlers after the troops left. Around Christmas 1853 Sarah Morgan had taken her infant son, Jacob, with her to visit her neighbors. On her way back home, a Comanche war party began chasing her.

Sarah looked over her shoulder at the painted faces of the warriors and knew she had to cross the Hamilton Creek Bridge to reach safety. Her husband would be riding out to meet her there. She had driven the same road many times in the past few months, and the Indians hadn't bothered her.

Jacob's cries had alerted the war party. She whipped the horses to make them run faster. Then she reached down to try to hush Jacob. The baby, frightened, cried even louder.

When she reached the curve before the bridge leading to Fort Croghan, Sarah reached down again to comfort her crying baby. She lost the reins and control of the horses. Running scared, the horses veered off the road and headed straight for the creek. When they rounded the curve, the wagon tongue snapped, leaving Sarah and the baby in the runaway wagon. It plunged off a ten-foot drop into the icy creek.

The Indians sat on their horses, watching the woman trying to save her baby from drowning. Laughing, they took turns shooting at her hands while she tried to hold her child out of the water. The baby's cries grew weaker each time it came up for air. Finally, Sarah grabbed hold of the baby's gown and pulled it up, holding it out of the water.

About the same time she pulled the child out of the water, a bullet hit the child in the chest; its blood covered Sarah's hands. Her screams echoed off the water and the timbers around the creek. Only when the warriors emptied cartridges into Sarah's numbed body did her screams die on the winds.

Sarah's husband heard her screams from the confines of Fort Croghan, where he had been doing some business at the trading post. Mounting his horse, he spurred the animal into a dead run toward Hamilton Creek Bridge. He was supposed to ride to the bridge to meet her, but thinking she would probably be late, he had tarried.

He came too late to save her or the baby. He arrived just in time to see the Indians riding off into the trees. Seeing the wagon parts strewn on the banks and floating in the creek, he dove into the water to try to save the child and its mother. Finding both of them dead, he buried them on the bank of Hamilton Creek.

Visitors to the partially reconstructed Fort Croghan have heard Sarah's cries for help and her baby's last gurgling breaths echo across the water's surface. To reach the Fort Croghan museum, start at 703 Buchanan Drive in Burnet. The museum is operated from April through mid-October, Thursday, Friday, and Saturday from 10:00 a.m. to 5:00 p.m. To reach the fort from Burnet, go west on State Highway 29. There is free parking on the grounds and in front of the museum.

CAMP CHARLOTTE

In a desolate area of Irion County, some local folks have reported several soldiers spurring their horses into action at the shot of a pistol. They charge across the dusty land near Camp Charlotte, their horses jumping the smaller brush and trees to weave their way in and out of the larger vegetation.

They race, shouting and having a good time until one horse and rider breaks from the crowd. A small young lady with long blonde hair rides a beautiful golden horse whose mane and tail are flying. The horse and rider fly across the ground.

Suddenly, the horse stumbles and begins to fall in slow motion. When they hit the ground, they disappear into the dust of the late afternoon at the confluence of Kiowa Creek and the Middle Concho River.

Like most forts on the Texas frontier, Camp Charlotte, a Civil War–era installation, was established to protect the Butterfield

Overland Mail routes against the Indians of the area. The troops built the stockade in April 1858 according to their instructions, making it a 115-foot by 190-foot rectangle and placing the officers' quarters and the guardhouse outside the walls of the garrison.

A small settlement grew up around the compound, and until the middle 1870s, the cavalry kept the mail stages and the settlers safe and happy. It was after the cavalry left that the Indian raids began again.

The small settlement often held a trader's market day at the post for the settlers and the soldiers to enjoy. The farmers and their wives brought preserved goods and animals to sell and trade with other farmers, therefore the money from the Camp Charlotte soldiers provided economic growth for the community.

One particular market day, the army sutlery and the trading post decided to sponsor a horse race. They spread the word to the settlers around the area; the two establishments were offering household goods, clothes, and shoes along with one special prize, a crystal chandelier, to the winner of the race. Young and old alike brought their horses to town for the event, hoping to win the prizes displayed at the trading post.

Everyone enjoyed the day and the late autumn breezes brought by cooler weather. Spirits ran high among the riders and their mounts. The riders became extra quiet while they waited for the lineup call. One rider in particular stood out. No one had ever seen the beautiful palomino filly, and each man wondered who the rider was, sitting huddled, terribly small, on the big horse.

Charlie Mason sat with her big floppy hat pulled low over her face, hiding her eyes. She held the filly's reins in gloved hands. She wanted the bundle of prizes for her family, especially the chandelier for her mother. Their family was poor and her mother never asked for anything, but Charlie knew she would love such a gorgeous adornment for her home.

She held her filly in check at the end of the mob of racers, the rest of whom were farmers, a few soldiers, and the younger boys of the area. She could ride as well as most of them and better than some.

Charlie had sneaked out of the house early to ride her horse the seven miles into town alone. The coolness of the day and the anticipation of the race made the lonely miles go by faster than she had thought they would. While waiting in town for the race to begin, she had tied the filly out of sight and roamed the vendor's setups. She spied several baskets of vegetables and fruits from neighboring farmers' gardens, but thought her mother's produce was much larger and of better quality. She listened to the yarns of some of the old men who sat gathered around telling of fights with different Indians and bandits.

Waiting for the race to begin, she was determined not to give in to the fearful, nagging feelings in the back of her mind. The rules of the race hadn't said anything about the rider having to be a man or boy. You had to have the fastest horse. There was nothing else in the rules about the riders.

The starter held his pistol into the air. His finger rested on the trigger and began to slowly pull it back. Charlie leaned over the filly's neck; no need being unseated with her fast takeoff. The explosion of the pistol burst the quiet of the peaceful settlement.

The shouts of the crowd were lost in the thunder of hooves when the horses lunged into action. The beginning of the race began evenly and as impressive as any cavalry charge against bandits or Indians.

Charlie and her filly flew alongside the rest of the racers for a scant quarter of a mile when some of the horses began to fade to the rear of the pack. Charlie's filly stayed in front, legging it close to the lead. More and more of the men and their horses dropped back until only four were left in contention for the prizes.

Charlie and three others raced for the finish line at the trading post. Edging out in front, Charlie forgot her anonymity and yanked the hat from her head to fan the filly's haunches to get more speed out of her. Charlie's long blonde hair flew wild in the wind, mingling with the mane of the filly. Thrown off balance by the sight of the young girl in the race, the men lost their train of concentration for the split second it took for Charlie and her filly to gain a good lead. Quickly the men recovered and chased after the girl and her yellow horse.

Charlie won the race in the cool autumn afternoon, but on the way home, she lost another. A small band of Kiowa Indians lay in wait along the mail route for the stage. When Charlie came around the curve with her beautiful filly and bundle of prizes, the Indians gave chase.

The filly, still full of energy, was easy to urge into a run, but her heart wasn't up to the added exertion and it burst. The filly stumbled to her knees and fell head over heels, throwing Charlie from the saddle. The filly and Charlie died when they hit the ground. The Kiowas gathered up the clothing and left the chandelier lying in the dirt. They took the saddle from the horse, and they cut Charlie's hair from her head.

The next morning the young girl and her horse were found where they'd died. The settlement mourned the young team's death. They had stolen the hearts of those who'd watched them race.

Now Charlie and her yellow filly race the wind and tumbleweeds across the flat prairie land near where Camp Charlotte once stood.

In the mid-1870s, infantry soldiers were hard put to protect the area against raiding Indians, but the small community around Camp Charlotte survived for a while.

In 1885, a post office was established and served the settlement until 1899 when the office was moved to San Angelo. Nothing except a historical marker remains of Camp Charlotte. Visitors to Irion County can see this marker about forty-five miles west of San Angelo, Texas, on the west side of State Highway 163.

PART IV

FORTS ESTABLISHED FROM 1866 TO PRESENT DAY

FORT RICHARDSON

Driving a lonely stretch of road between Jacksboro and Mineral Wells, Texas, a couple of young women had a blowout on the rear tire of their automobile. Having no other choice, they started walking to the nearest farm or town. They hadn't walked far when they heard the *clip-clopping* of hooves behind them. The girls turned, and there stood a huge, raw-boned bay horse, his body covered with scars. One girl, Kit, being an experienced rider, caught the rein around the horse's neck and looked it over. The horse stood stock-still, as if waiting for her to give a command.

"Well, at least we won't have to walk anymore. We'll bring him back when we get a new tire put on the car." Kit leapt up on the horse's back and held her hand down to Laurie.

Taking only half the time to get back to Jacksboro, the girls rode up to a station that had tires for sale. They tied the horse to a rack and went inside.

The girls told the man at the service counter that they needed a tire for their car, explaining they had left the car several miles in the country and had ridden in on a horse they found.

"Horse?" The man looked curiously out the window.

"Yes, he's tied to the rack outside."

The Fort Richardson headquarters building stands waiting to invite visitors to the old fort.

"No horse there now." The man grinned and continued looking at tire charts.

The girls rushed to the door and looked at the empty rack. The horse was gone. They expressed their concern about not being able to return the horse to its owner.

The man chuckled. "Don't worry about that horse. He doesn't have an owner. In fact, he was never really there. What you rode in on, ladies, was a ghost horse."

The man told them the story of the old fort and the horse. Fort Richardson was first established to replace Fort Belknap. It began life in 1866 as Fort Buffalo Springs some thirty miles north of the present location. In 1867 it was relocated near Lost Creek and renamed Fort Richardson in 1868.

In the late 1860s whorehouses and saloons sprang up in "Sudsville," a nearby settlement, where most soldiers from the fort spent their time off. However, in the 1870s Indian attacks forced the troops to earn their pay. They had to learn the hand-to-hand combat tactics of Indian warfare to stay alive and protect the settlers.

In 1871 there was a massacre of a wagon train bringing supplies to the fort the day after Gen. William T. Sherman traveled the same road. The Kiowa medicine man, De-ha-te, told the Indians about the wagons coming, so they did not attack Sherman's entourage. The attack took place on Salt Creek Prairie about twenty-two miles from Fort Richardson. Only a few of the drivers escaped the brutal murders committed by the Kiowas that day.

General Sherman promised the settlers he would put a stop to the brutality of the Indians. He took immediate action and hunted down the three chiefs: Satank, Big Tree, and Satanta. Satank was killed on the way to justice after he attacked his guards.

In July 1875 twenty-six Texas Rangers tracked a war party and caught up with them west of Fort Richardson. The commanding officer had to send back to the fort for reinforcements because the Indians had grown in strength to one hundred and outnumbered the twenty-six rangers, who only had fourteen horses left. The odds of winning that battle were not good. Troops were sent to the rangers' aid, and the Indians disappeared into the scenery.

During this stretch of war, Colonel Mackenzie learned that a Comanche without a horse was defeatable. He learned to be ruthless and quick in his strategy. Retreat and repeat were the tactics most used by the Comanches and other tribes, and Mackenzie adapted his lessons well. The Indian-fighting techniques he had learned while he was commander at Fort Richardson led him to command the troops who fought in Palo Duro Canyon in 1874. Many Indians died at Palo Duro Canyon as well as many soldiers, but there were many who returned to fight another day.

In the spring of 1871, while Colonel Mackenzie was encountering Quanah Parker, a teamster was about to deal with his own Indian problem.

Uneasy, Thomas Brazeal, riding shotgun on a supply wagon headed for Fort Richardson, looked around at the dense trees surrounding the wagon train. He knew the Indians were there; he could feel it. He had earlier mentioned his feeling of foreboding to others in the caravan, but they brushed it aside.

The supplies in the wagons were a temptation to the Indians, one too great for them to pass up. He convinced himself that the only way to stay alive was to stay alert and keep an eye out for Kiowas.

The first war cry from the Kiowas caught most of the teamsters by surprise, but Thomas was prepared. He jumped from the wagon seat into the back where he had prepared a hiding place that morning before they broke camp. Sitting low in the wagon, he was concealed, and he could fire with a fair amount of accuracy if he took as much time as possible to aim.

"Hank," Thomas shouted to the driver, "get under the seat! Don't give those devils a target."

The warning was barely out of his mouth when he saw Hank pitch forward from the wagon, an arrow in his throat. With no one at the reins, the team of horses stampeded across the prairie, dragging the wagon over rocks, ruts, and tree stumps. Thomas knew he'd either have to jump or be killed if the wagon flipped over.

Still firing rapidly, he stood in the careening wagon and took stock of the passing ground, looking for a place to jump. Seeing a small grassy slope, he jumped, reminding himself to roll when he hit the ground. He landed with a yell as pain tore into his knee. Rolling, he doubled his knees as close to his chest as he could and tried to hold onto his rifle. When he rolled up against an outcropping covered with mesquite brush, his rifle skittered several feet away from him. Lying still in the shelter of brush, he assessed the wound in his leg.

Thomas heard several more wagons roll by, then watched as the Kiowa braves overtook the teams, one by one, and captured the teamsters who hadn't already been killed. He waited, partially hidden under the mesquites. Apparently the Indians had overlooked him as they rode swiftly past, intent on the men they could readily see.

Thomas huddled close to the ground, watching the braves slash at the corpses of his fellow teamsters. Brutally, they bashed in the skulls of men already dead and then shot more arrows into their bodies. Seeing firsthand the savagery the Kiowa were capable of, Thomas prayed they would not find him.

After the pleasure of desecrating the dead waned, the Indians turned to the captives. The bloodlust in their eyes told Thomas that the others were lucky to be dead.

Thomas watched as the savages dragged a half-conscious Jack Elms to the fire. Thomas fought against the instinct to rush forward and go to the aid of his friend, but caution forced him back into his hiding place. Tears of helplessness trickled down his face as several Kiowa held Jack while another cut out his tongue.

The sun was low above the treetops when the Indians chained Jack to a wagon tongue and set up stakes over a fire. Like a side of beef, they hefted Jack and the wagon tongue upon the stakes and roasted him alive. Thomas held his hands over his ears, trying to shut out the horrible guttural sounds of the dying man. With darkness upon them, they quickly slaughtered the other teamsters and settled down to sleep.

Thomas knew his only chance was in getting to Fort Richardson, but to manage that in the darkness with a broken leg would take a miracle.

The miracle came in the form of a huge bay horse. Thomas felt a hot breath on his neck. Then he felt the velvety muzzle and turned to see the bay's nose. One of the Indians' horses snuffled quietly at him, and then backed away a couple of steps. His prayers had been answered.

"Whoa, boy, don't go away." Thomas crooned softly to the horse while crawling toward it. Slowly he caught its leg, talking to the bay all the while. Pulling himself to his feet, he tugged a rawhide strap over the bay's head for a rein. Thomas turned the horse away from the bright light of the campfire, careful not to be seen by the Indians standing watch.

He pulled himself onto the horse's back and lay over its neck, flattening against the animal as much as possible. Thomas urged the bay out into the darkness, trying not to be noticed. A sudden cry from a Kiowa brave brought flying arrows Thomas's way. Before reaching the protection of the brush and heavy darkness, an arrow pierced Thomas's good leg, continuing deep into the horse's ribs. Miraculously, the horse remained on its feet and continued to run as Thomas clung to its neck and mane.

Reaching Fort Richardson, Thomas was taken to the hospital for treatment. From his sickbed, he begged the troops who cared for him to also tend to the horse and keep it safe. The bay had rescued him and deserved the best treatment possible. Thomas spoke with General Sherman and told the officer of the depredations he'd witnessed against the other teamsters. Thomas again asked that his mount be cared for and its life saved. The big bay horse apparently had no intentions of dying. His wound quickly, almost miraculously, healed. Each day he stood, looking toward the hospital, as if waiting for Thomas to come for him.

But Thomas Brazeal died, and the horse became the property of the US Army.

Terrance, a young wrangler, took a shine to the big bay horse. After acquiring permission to take the bay as his mount, the two quickly became a team. Terrance and the bay were assigned to ride out with the detail sent to transport the three chiefs, Satanta, Big Tree, and Satank, at Fort Sill, Kansas, back to Fort Richardson.

On the return trip the bay was badly wounded again when Satank jumped from the wagon and attacked Terrance. Satank cut the horse as well as Terrance. The cut along the bay's neck bled profusely, causing the horse to become too weak to be ridden. The cut on Terrance's arm went deep, and he was forced to ride in the supply wagon back to Fort Richardson.

One of the officers started to put the bay down, but Terrance talked him out of shooting the animal, hoping the horse had enough stamina to get back to the fort, where he could be cared for properly. Terrance tied the bay to the back of the wagon for the trip home, where once again the horse cheated death.

By the end of the march to Fort Richardson, the tribes of the Texas plains had heard of the horse that wouldn't die. Many attempts were made by the Indians to steal the bay horse, but all failed.

When young Terrance returned to duty, he and the bay rode along with Colonel Mackenzie on the raid at Palo Duro Canyon, where Terrance died of wounds received in battle. The raw-boned horse returned to Fort Richardson with yet another rider and another wound. Time and time again the horse was wounded, but none of the wounds he received took his life. He carried Corporal Terrance's friend for a couple of years longer.

One evening, after a ride into Sudsville, the horse stood tied in front of the saloon, waiting for the return of his new owner. A young man who had too much to drink stepped out of the saloon, shooting his pistol in celebration. A stray bullet apparently ricocheted off the target, striking the horse in the head. The bay fell dead in his tracks. When night descended over the town, the soldier hired some men to bury the horse as he had promised Corporal Terrance before he died.

After that the soldier was afoot. The man whose bullet killed the horse was ordered to replace the army mount, but the soldier never developed a good relationship with that horse. It could never be the same as riding the bay.

Many times folks tell of being stranded when, out of the blue, a big bay horse is seen standing nearby, waiting to give a lift to anyone who needs it. The horse has been seen several times along Lost Creek, near Fort Richardson. His body is scarred from the wounds he received, and he isn't much to look at, but his eyes are gentle and he is a friend to anyone in need.

The autumn and winter of 1874 and 1875 saw the last of the Indian wars in Texas and signaled the end of the need for Fort Richardson. The fort was closed on March 29, 1878, and by May all the troops were gone. To visit Fort Richardson, drive south on State Highway 281/199 to the Jacksboro city limits. The fort is at 228 State Park Road 61, Jacksboro. It is open seven days a week.

FORT GRIFFIN

Along the Clear Fork of the Brazos below the mesa where Fort Griffin stood, a beautiful voice can be heard. It belongs to Sara Rose, who drowned in the Brazos after being molested by several men from the "Flat." Sara Rose's voice wafts over the winds blowing up to the Fort Griffin mesa before flying away.

On the Clear Fork of the Brazos, four companies of the Sixth Cavalry established Fort Griffin at the end of July 1867. First built on the river, the army relocated it to the top of the hundred-foot-high mesa above the river.

A small community called the "Flat," lying at the base of the mesa, sprang up and figured strongly in the annals of the history of Fort Griffin. Lonely soldiers from the fort often frequented the saloons in search of whiskey and the pleasure of the "girls" working there. Such famous men as Doc Holliday, Bat Masterson, and Wyatt Earp were also known to visit the saloons of the "Flat."

Fort Griffin's troops were well known as men who would fight with anyone. These were the soldiers who supported all the major battles with the Indians from the late 1860s to the late 1880s. The troops of Fort Griffin not only fought hard, they played hard, and everyone in Texas knew it.

One soldier in particular, called Curly by his friends, often rode down from Fort Griffin mesa to see a certain pretty young woman named Sara Rose, who sang in one of the saloons. Curly and Sara Rose could be seen together every day he wasn't out on patrol. They walked and talked, making future plans, and like a couple of kids in love they played.

Sara Rose had been stranded at the "Flat" when her drunken husband had been killed one night when others had caught him cheating at poker. Penniless and desperate, Sara Rose agreed to sing

Most of Fort Griffin is in ruins, like this former administration building.

for the soldiers and other rowdies who visited the saloon. With her fresh, innocent beauty, she could have profited greatly, but she was adamant to the owner and absolutely refused to accompany the soldiers upstairs. Her aloofness only served in making her all the more desirable to the men. The soldiers weren't the only men taken with her beauty. Others, including the enticingly handsome Wyatt Earp and his friend, Doc Holliday, competed for Sara Rose's smile.

In spite of all the attention she received, Sara Rose kept to herself, until she met Curly. His gentle manners, boyish smile, and soft curls melted her heart. She fell deeply in love with the tall, blue-eyed soldier.

Their love deepened and soon Curly proposed, but he wanted to wait to be married until his discharge from the army came about, so he could take his bride to his home.

Sara Rose agreed to wait, and in the meantime, in order to make a living for herself, she had to continue singing at the saloon.

To save Sara Rose from having to live in quarters over the saloon, Curly built her a tiny cabin near their favorite spot on the

Clear Fork River. When he wasn't on patrol, he and Sara would have their picnic lunches beside the water.

After she finished work at night, Curly usually waited there to protect her on the walk home. If he was on duty, he arranged for a friend to accompany her in his stead.

One night neither Curly nor his friend was at the saloon when Sara Rose finished for the night, and she started for her cabin alone when several men from the "Flat" abruptly surrounded her. Rowdy and boisterous, they insisted on escorting her home. She politely refused, but the men were drunk and would not take no for an answer.

Out of earshot of anyone who might help her, one of the men held her hands behind her back while another held her mouth open and poured whiskey into her mouth. The men took turns with Sara Rose in the bedroom of her cabin. When they finished with her, they left her crying for Curly.

Sara stumbled through the tiny house, straightening the furniture the drunken men had turned over; she cleaned her home and stripped the sheets from her bed. Tossing them into the fireplace, she burned the soiled sheets. Feeling unclean herself, she went down to the river to wash away the horror.

Sara Rose was never seen alive again.

The next morning, her bludgeoned, half-clothed body was found floating on the muddy waters of the Clear Fork of the Brazos.

Brokenhearted, Curly buried Sara Rose under a sprawling tree where they had sat on long summer evenings. Unable to deal with the brutality of her death and the loss of his beloved, he volunteered to go west and join another troop.

Sara Rose's voice can still be heard sometimes at night, singing for her lost love. On some evenings in the bend of the Brazos, the sound drifts up toward the ruins of Fort Griffin to blend with the birds' songs and the chirping of the crickets. Some have seen her on the path that once led to the small cabin. Others have seen her walking along the banks of the river.

The remnants of a foundation are all that's left of this former officers' quarters at Fort Griffin.

Fort Griffin was established in July 1867, and after the Civil War the army reoccupied the fort with four companies of the Sixth Cavalry of the United States. During the 1877 buffalo-hunting season, more than two hundred thousand hides were shipped east from Fort Griffin, and the soldiers had to keep the peace among the buffalo hunters and the Indians.

When the buffalo were killed off, the focus of the area around Fort Griffin turned to cattle. The Kansas quarantine of Texas cattle down through Fort Worth caused a bitter war of words between local newspapers. When the cattle trail to San Antonio came to be diverted through Fort Griffin, once again the soldiers were called upon to keep the peace in the area.

Later, Fort Griffin needed law and order—crime ran rampant and citizens finally saw something had to be done. This happened in many lawless boom towns and Fort Griffin was no exception. The citizens seemed to think the only answer was to form a citizen's committee to the law. No matter what they called it, the citizens often became mobs and were then known as vigilantes.

In Fort Griffin, the violence grew so fast and furious that a vigilante group called the OLM, or Old Law Mob, was formed. Members met, made up a list of the undesirables in the town, and posted it in saloons and around the town. Those on the list were warned to leave town or else. After a short time period if those listed were still in town they were taken into custody and either shot to death or hung from the nearest tree. The citizens posted the letters "OLM" on the bodies for all to see and as a warning to those still on the list.

Another event in Fort Griffin's history occurred when the Texas Rangers moved their base of operations to Camp Sibley. The railroad went through Abilene and Albany, causing the demise of Fort Griffin. In 1881, when the army abandoned Fort Griffin, the "Flat" also slipped slowly into history, and the last store closed its doors in the late 1950s.

Drifters and riffraff who occupied the town at the foot of the mesa left soon after Fort Griffin was closed. For the fourteen-year period of the fort's operation, the town named "Flat" grew famous for its many Wild West characters: Wyatt Earp, John H. "Doc" Holliday, Bat Masterson, and lesser gunslingers. John Selman, Pat Garrett, "Big Nose" Kate Elder, "The Poker Queen" Lottie Deno, and many fallen angels walked its streets, leaving their marks on the town like dust on the pages of history.

Remnants of Fort Griffin are now on the grounds of a state historic site. It is also home to the Official State of Texas Longhorn Herd. The park offers camping, fishing, hiking, stargazing, and living history.

Among the fort's ruins are a mess hall, barracks, first sergeant's quarters, bakery, powder magazine, and a hand-dug well that tied Fort Griffin and Albany to Texas history. The campgrounds are located on the banks of the Clear Fork of the Brazos River. It provides visitors with an opportunity to relax under the large shade trees, enjoy the playground, catch catfish in the river, or hike nature trails to the campground. Because of the vast ranches surrounding the property, Fort Griffin has minimal light pollution. This results as an astronomer's oasis with great skies for viewing constellations, planets, and galaxies at Fort Griffin's monthly stargazing events.

Fort Griffin is also a State Archeological Landmark and listed in the National Register of Historic Places.

The remains of Fort Griffin can be visited thirteen miles north of Albany in Shackelford County on US Highway 283. The park is open daily from 8:00 a.m. to 4:30 p.m. except Thanksgiving Day, Christmas Eve, Christmas Day, New Year's Eve, and New Year's Day. Entrance fees to the park are four dollars per day/person for adults and three dollars per day/person for students (ages six to eighteen). No admission is charged for children ages five and younger. Admission for school groups is one dollar per student (reservations required), and guided tours are seven dollars per adult and six dollars per student (ages six to eighteen). Fort Griffin offers overnight camping for a fee at thirty-three campsites and primitive camping on nearly five acres.

FORT CONCHO

In the homes on Officers Row at Fort Concho, a young girl of ten to twelve years old is often seen playing jacks in the upstairs hall or in the right-hand bedroom. When the child is about, the temperature in the room is substantially cooler. She doesn't say much if anyone sees her. She'll smile and go on playing, but when you turn your back or look again, she will be gone. The child's father, Col. Benjamin H. Grierson, one of the former commanders at Fort Concho, lived in the house during his command.

In Grierson's old quarters, a florist had an interesting tale about a delivery he'd made. He'd knocked and when a lady answered the door, he asked where she wanted the first batch of flowers placed. He retrieved two large bouquets of gardenias and peace lilies from his van and returned to the house.

"The lilies go in the bedroom to the right at the top of the stairs. The gardenias go in the room on the left."

Taking the two large bouquets up the stairs, he noticed how much cooler the stairwell and second floor were than the first floor. Entering the bedroom on the right, he nearly tripped over a small girl around ten or twelve years old.

"Excuse me."

She never looked up from her game of jacks. Shrugging, he went on about his business, arranging the flowers on the bedside table, and then he went into the other upstairs bedroom to place the flowers where the lady had instructed. Before leaving the upstairs, he peeked back into the first bedroom and saw the girl had left. The flowers had been moved to a table in the corner, and the child's jacks were on the bedside table. The florist smiled. The flowers did look better in the corner anyway, and he left them where the child had put them. Besides, she would obviously be staying in the room for the weekend with her parents.

After finishing upstairs, he then filled the rooms downstairs with the flowers and didn't see the girl again. He brought in the last of the delivery and noticed a picture hanging above the fireplace to be the likeness of the child he had seen in the bedroom.

"You have such a charming daughter. It was extremely nice of the staff here at Fort Concho to allow you to hang her portrait above the fireplace while you are staying here." He pointed to the picture and wondered where the child had gone.

"Oh," the lady said, "I don't have any children. The girl in that portrait is the daughter of Col. Benjamin H. Grierson, regimental commanding officer of the 10th Cavalry. Her name was Edith, and she died in the bedroom upstairs around her twelfth birthday."

"I saw her playing in the bedroom when I took the flowers up there, and she even moved them after I arranged them."

Chuckling, the lady informed the florist, "I am not laughing at you, but Edith is often seen playing in her room. Others have seen her about the house as well."

While visiting Fort Concho, I entered the officers' quarters where Edith stays. I felt her presence when I started up the stairs.

The air blasting from the bedroom on the right at the top of the stairs felt much colder than the air in the bedroom on the left or on the first floor. When I entered into the living room where Edith's portrait hangs above the fireplace, the air was again several degrees colder than in the rest of the house. Edith definitely made herself known upon my entry into her home.

Edith is present year-round, unlike other ghostly beings at Fort Concho who mostly come around in December.

During preparations for the Christmas show in December for the first time, a presence was detected in another of the officers' quarters. A staff member at Fort Concho heard footsteps behind her in the building. When she turned to see who might be in the room with her, she reported a blast of cold air that literally knocked her up against the wall. Terribly frightened, she said she heard the unique sound of knuckles cracking. This was a well-known habit of Col. Ranald S. Mackenzie, the officer who took the troops to Palo Duro Canyon to fight the Indians on their own grounds. More than one of the staff members believe the ghost of Colonel Mackenzie still lurks at Fort Concho.

While I walked from the hospital to the officers' quarters, I had the uncanny feeling of someone watching me. I looked around and saw no one, but then my eye caught a shadowy movement in an upstairs window of the officers' quarters where Colonel Mackenzie once lived. After reaching the porch of the one particular building, I found it padlocked and no one visible inside.

When I mentioned the incident to one of the fort personnel, I was told it was more than likely the colonel, who had been sighted at this particular house more than once.

The house where I saw the shadow had been the home of Colonel Mackenzie and his family during his stay at Fort Concho. Apparently he became quite fond of the centrally located house because it gave him a full view of everything happening around the fort, including the stone corral where the Indian women and children were housed after their capture at Palo Duro Canyon.

On one occasion, staff members watching the grounds from the headquarters building saw a male figure in the upstairs window of the officers' quarters next to the Mackenzie house. He wore a light blue shirt with his sleeves rolled up to his elbows.

A tour guide stood on the porch, unlocking the door in order to take a group inside. Watching through binoculars, one staff member said the officer in the window scowled, as if the tour group was going to interrupt his activities. The guide opened the door, and the ghostly figure stepped away from the window and disappeared into the shadows.

What was probably the spirit of Fort Concho's Chaplain Dunbar and possibly an officer's wife were overheard discussing how something had to be done at the chapel building near the hospital. The lady apparently said, "Chaplain Dunbar, it should be done like this."

No one knows what the two were talking about, and Chaplain Dunbar's response was never heard. It had taken four or five years and many plans to convince the army of the need for the church/schoolhouse. It took even longer to get it built after the chaplain received approval. The staff member who overheard the conversation prefers to think the two were talking about the plans for building the chapel.

The first time anyone from the ghostly world became evident in the headquarters building came on a Sunday afternoon. The staff had finished up their first annual "First Weekend of December" celebration. In order to be ready for each day's activities, a staff member had spent the weekend in an upstairs room of the old headquarters building. Late one Sunday evening, while she packed her gear to leave and go home, the lights started flickering off and on. She tried to reach the bulb to unscrew it without a ladder. She couldn't reach it. She flipped the switch, but it kept switching off and on. Turning off the power didn't help either.

She finally gave up and said, "Okay, Sarge, I am leaving now. I'll be back next year." The lights quit blinking, and when she turned the switch off, the lights stayed off.

The next unusual incident at the headquarters occurred the next Christmas season at the fort, the first weekend of December. In the adjutant's office at the far end of the fort, the lights again flashed off and on, but this time a lamp hanging from the ceiling began to rotate. The same staff member from the year before spoke to the sergeant.

"Sergeant Fletcher, we are only going to be here one or two days. The same as last year."

The fixture continued to swing in a revolving motion. In the next room, another light fixture began moving back and forth while the first lamp swung in its circular path. Calling a fellow staff member, she asked if they saw anything unusual. The second staff member confirmed the strange occurrences.

The second staff member spoke up. "If you are Sergeant Fletcher, swing this lamp." She pointed to a lamp in the second room they had entered. The lamp swung straight at her with great force, barely missing her head. Again, they told the ghost they would be leaving shortly, and the light fixtures abruptly stopped moving.

A couple of years later, it was decided that Sergeant Fletcher, who had been stationed at Fort Concho, didn't like women in the headquarters buildings. The staff assumes Sergeant Fletcher considers himself to be the protector of the building.

While I stood in the headquarters building, the tour guide told me that he has heard the heavy sound of boots on the porch at each of the barracks buildings. The first time he got up to look and see if someone had been sent to take the tour. It puzzled him because no one from the office had called to tell him they were sending someone down, and no one stood or walked on the porch. He feels strongly that it is the ghost of Sergeant Cunningham, an Irish trooper who died of cholera in the barracks. Sergeant Cunningham, not wanting to die alone in the hospital, asked to be taken to the barracks in order to die among his men.

The enlisted men's quarters at Fort Concho is where you might encounter the ghost of Sergeant Fletcher.

Soldiers established Fort Concho at the junction of the North and Middle Concho Rivers in 1867. Like many other Texas frontier forts, the government built Fort Concho to protect the settlers and transportation routes. Company H of the Fourth US Cavalry under the command of Capt. George Gibson Huntt rode into the Concho Valley in December to stabilize the area.

Although flat and treeless prairie surrounded it, Fort Concho was reported to be "one of the most beautiful and best ordered posts in Texas." Obviously Fort Concho had been built with taste and elegance in mind as well as convenience. Private landowners leased out the land to the government, and the stonemasons who built the fort's structures were private citizens who traveled from Fredericksburg to do the work.

By 1879 the eight companies of troops who defended the fort lived in the forty permanent buildings and a number of temporary structures. The post had a garden to help supply food for the soldiers and their families, and they hunted buffalo and turkey occasionally to supplement the diets of the men.

Such commanders as William Shafter, Ranald S. Mackenzie, Benjamin H. Grierson, John P. Hatch, and Wesley Merritt took responsibility for the troops that included each of the four Buffalo Soldier units. Fort Concho also served the Tenth US Cavalry headquartered from 1875 to 1882, the Fourth US Cavalry between 1868 and 1873, the Eleventh US Infantry in 1870, and the Sixteenth US Cavalry from 1882 until 1887.

In the early years of Fort Concho's existence, the troopers fought with many of the small bands of Indians in the area. Colonel Mackenzie's campaign in 1872, the Red River War, and the Victoria Campaign of 1879–1880 saw Fort Concho supplying not only goods to keep the troops going, but also troops.

In 1872 and 1873 more than a hundred Indian women and children were held captive at Fort Concho. For six months they lived in the stone corrals there. On June 20, 1889, Fort Concho was officially abandoned because it had ceased to be of any value to the area since Indian attacks were no longer a threat. The buildings escaped being torn down because the settlers took up residence in the officers' quarters. Merchants from San Angelo used some of the stone structures for storage buildings.

Fort Concho had a very large hospital to care for the sick and wounded.

The city of San Angelo began taking an interest in the preservation of the old fort and acquired the land where Fort Concho stood in 1935 after a museum had already been started there. They began restoring the buildings, and Fort Concho became a National Landmark in 1961, with further plans for reconstruction to begin in 1967. Reconstruction and land acquisitions continue today.

Fort Concho is located at the corner of Oakes and Avenue D in San Angelo, off US Highway 277 out of Abilene. There are self-guided and guided tours available. The facility is open Monday through Saturday from 9:00 a.m. to 4:30 p.m. Admission is $3.00 for adults, $2.00 for seniors and military, $1.50 for children ages seven to seventeen, and free for children age six and younger. Guided tour prices are slightly higher.

CAMP ELIZABETH

Driving out of San Angelo north on US Highway 183, there are times when one might catch a glimpse of a beautiful blonde lady riding a huge black horse. She will smile as she passes you in her green velvet riding habit and her big floppy cavalry hat. If you look twice, you won't see her a second time. She rides like the wind and disappears among the tumbleweeds to ride again another day.

Taken over in 1874 by Fort Concho after the Texas Rangers established the post in 1853, Camp Elizabeth served mainly as an outpost hospital and was used to teach horsemanship to the Buffalo Soldiers.

Camp Elizabeth sported officers' quarters, a hospital, a farrier's shop, and rock corrals. Most of the enlisted troops slept in tents near the officers' quarters. Springs on the North Concho River supplied the water for the camp. Near that spring is where Charlotte Sue in her green dress may be seen riding her black horse among the tumbleweeds of the prairie.

As a young girl, Miss Charlotte Sue Elizabeth Cross, hailing from a prominent family in the East, left her home to find adventure in the West. She resented the restraints placed on women by society. Stealing her brother's clothes, she dressed like a boy and took the horse her father had given her for her birthday. He had allowed her to ride only occasionally. Charlotte cut her long blonde hair and called herself Charles. Traveling as far west as Fort Concho, she joined the army and was immediately placed into the cavalry because she had her own horse.

Charlotte could ride only well enough not to lose her balance. She was sent to Camp Elizabeth, where inexperienced soldiers were taught horsemanship. Charlotte spent many hours in the saddle during her stay at Camp Elizabeth. She learned how to ride well, and she quickly mastered all the required skills of a cavalryman.

In the meantime, Charlotte Sue began to blossom as a woman, and it became increasingly hard to conceal what she didn't want the army or anyone else to know. Thankfully, she shared a tent with no one else. Her hair grew longer and became more and more difficult to keep under her hat. Hating the short locks, she bowed to her female vanity and resisted cutting it again. The feminine facial features she had drew attention from the other men because she never had to shave. It seemed like the more exercise she got, the more her body curves told of signs of trouble to come. To make matters worse, she fell in love with a young officer in command.

Late one evening after everyone in the company was asleep, Charlotte Sue, determined to follow her heart and her womanly ways, donned a dress she had been hiding in her footlocker. Folding her army uniform neatly, she placed it on the bed but took her floppy cavalry hat and plopped it on her head. Composing a note, she explained to the young officer whose affections she sought why she left, and then she told him of her feelings for him, adding, "It was a great way for me to get out and see a part of the world." She signed the note with her real name, Charlotte Sue Elizabeth Cross. She then left the camp, taking her horse with her.

Charlotte Sue rode out into the dark night and was never seen again. As soon as her note was found the next morning and after all recovered from the shock, the army sent out a search party to bring her back, but she was nowhere to be found. Soon after, only a few miles from Camp Elizabeth, a trooper found her hat.

What happened to Elizabeth will always remain a mystery. Some believe she made her way back home, but most believe she died, lost in the wilderness.

In 1886, Camp Elizabeth was permanently closed. Local citizens eventually tore down the remaining buildings.

Driving slowly along the highway where Camp Elizabeth once stood strangers have reported seeing a huge black horse running hard straight toward their vehicles. Some say they are mesmerized by the sight of the beautiful animal and the young woman riding it. She is usually dressed in a green velvet riding habit and a big floppy cavalry hat. Tendrils of her pale blonde hair flutter from under the hat. She never slows the horse. She urges him on as fast as he can run until they resemble a dust devil of wind blowing across the empty pastureland.

To visit the site where Camp Elizabeth once stood, from San Angelo take US Highway 183 north toward Big Spring. Camp Elizabeth is approximately nine miles northwest of Sterling City on US Highway 87, where a Texas historical monument stands.

FORT BUFFALO SPRINGS

Visitors to the ruins of Fort Buffalo Springs claim that if the wind blows exactly right, you are still able to hear the ghostly whoops and hollers of attacking Comanches. Among the bloodcurdling war cries, a few maintain they can pick out the voices of a few supernatural civilians shouting, "Help is on the way!" Then the wind shifts, and only the bobwhite calls and creaking windmills accompany the song of rustling leaves.

The settlement of Buffalo Springs came to life in 1864 when twenty-five families settled there to farm. Comanche attacks on their homes persisted, threatening the community. A brief reprise arrived in the form of the army, but the soldiers stayed only a short while.

The Sixth Cavalry's two companies, sent from Jacksboro in 1867, established and occupied Fort Buffalo Springs. Besides answering the settlers' need for protection, much like their counterparts at other forts on the Texas frontier, the troops also patrolled a wide area from Fort Belknap to Fort Phantom Hill. The soldiers arriving at Fort Buffalo Springs had orders to build structures for a permanent fort, but the water supply was as inadequate as the timber supply.

The fort was brand new when the main body of the regiment was called out on patrol to find a small war party wreaking havoc on settlers to the south of Jacksboro. A handful of troops were left to man Fort Buffalo Springs.

The regiment need not have gone far to seek out the Comanches. The war party sat on their horses atop a hill overlooking Fort Buffalo Springs and watched as the troopers rode away.

Two young boys near the fort who were plowing a field stopped to watch the troops leave, as well.

"Someday I'm going to be an Indian fighter," Jake announced.

"Pshaw," Eustas answered. "You know better than that. Your ma ain't going to let you out of her sight long enough to go fight Comanches."

"Eustas, you don't know anything, do you? When I get old enough, my ma can't tell me what I can and can't do."

"Well, I'll bet you beans to bacon she does. I know your ma and she ain't going to let you join no army."

The boys argued for the better part of a half an hour. Finally, when the sun reached the point high in the sky, they decided to sit under an oak and eat their lunches.

"Hey, Jake, look yonder. Ain't them Comanches?" Eustas pointed toward the horizon.

Jake shaded his eyes and strained to make out the distant shapes.

"Sure enough, Eustas. It's them heathens! We got to tell Pa. Come on."

The boys left their lunches on the ground, jumped onto the plow horse, and headed toward the cabin.

The boys told their fathers about the Comanches they had seen and then recounted the sight of the mass of soldiers they saw riding out earlier in the morning.

Jake's father clanged the warning bell to gather the men from the settlement and then organized a war party of his own. The farmers rigged up their wagons, buckboards, and oxcarts with pots, pans, and anything they thought could possibly make noise, loaded the wagons with their families, and started toward Fort Buffalo Springs.

About a quarter of a mile from the fort, the settlers came near enough to hear the war cries of the Comanches, and they countered by making their own noise. The men, women, and children banged on their pots, pans, and tubs, yelling and screaming.

Eustas yelled out, "Help is on its way!"

Confused about where the noise was corning from, the Comanches retreated into the countryside, scattering in the wind.

Though they were few in number, the soldiers didn't lose a single life in the skirmish with the Comanches, and they invited the settlers to stay until the main body of the regiment returned. The regiment returned the next week to find their beds full of settlers. The goodwill between soldiers and settlers endured, but the fort did not.

The drought and lack of wood, even more than the frequent Indian attacks, caused the fort to close. Fort Buffalo Springs was abandoned only a few months after its establishment in 1867.

The same obstacles dashed the settlers' dreams of farming, and they moved out as well. The families who had led the crazy attack on the Indians stayed only another month or two after the army moved to Jacksboro.

In later years, the Buffalo Springs settlement boasted a population of two hundred citizens, two cotton gins, several businesses, and numerous screaming phantoms.

In the 1990s, fewer than fifty residents remained, farming the land abandoned to the Comanches more than 130 years before. The spirits of those early farmers linger, though, to reciprocate once more if their protectors should need protection. North of Jacksboro, Texas, in Clay County, when the wind blows from the right direction, one might hear the ghostly heroic settlers of yesterday defending what they deemed precious, their lands and their lives. There are only memories to prove the existence of Fort Buffalo Springs and those long-ago settlers who came to the army's aid, but to witness the history, take FM 3077 fifteen miles south of Henrietta or thirty miles north of Jacksboro in Clay County.

FORT HANCOCK

Corporal Robinson's ghost is seen often by visitors to the Fort Hancock ruins, trudging through knee-deep water as he leads horses behind him. He'll walk through the water and vanish upon dry ground.

At other times, if a fire is raging around the area where Fort Hancock once stood, again Corporal Robinson will make an appearance, leading the horses and disappearing in a swirl of smoke.

Fort Hancock was established on April 15, 1881, to defend settlers against Indians and bandits from across the Rio Grande and to serve as a subpost of Fort Davis. Over a year later, on July 9, 1882, the army moved the fort six miles to a site on the Southern Pacific Railroad, northwest of Fort Quitman.

Commanding officer general William T. Sherman talked the US War Department into purchasing Fort Hancock. Due to its proximity to the railroad, General Sherman believed Fort Hancock would be a permanent installation.

The army purchased the land for Fort Hancock at a price of $2,370 in 1883. On July 17 of the same year, Congress authorized improvements to the fort at a cost of $47,000.

The first garrison of the independent post, Company I of the Tenth US Cavalry, led by Capt. Theodore A. Baldwin, was later joined by a mixture of detachments of infantry and cavalry numbering not more than sixty men at a time. The troops patrolled the Rio Grande for illegal crossings by smugglers, bandits, and insurrectionists.

Originally called Camp Rice, the post received a new name on May 14, 1886, to honor Maj. Gen. Winfield Scott Hancock after his death on February 9, 1886. Generally garrisoned by a mixture of troops from infantry and cavalry detachments, Fort Hancock served the army under several different commanders.

Flood and fire plagued Fort Hancock. Soldiers constructed dikes against the Rio Grande, but they tended to break, and floods were imminent in the lower sections of the fort.

At one point, heavy rains poured for several days, swelling the Rio Grande over its banks. The soldiers had worked day and night for weeks building a dike around Fort Hancock, hoping to hold the water from the interior of the compound, but the western levy was weak.

"I sure don't like this black water, Sam." Corporal Robinson shoveled two scoops of mud to his friend's one.

"Don't think about it. Just a lot of rain gathering up in one spot. That's what it is, Robinson."

"I still don't like it. If there's two things in this world I don't care for more than anything else, its raging waters and fires. Humans can't stop either one no matter how hard they try. You know God destroyed the earth with water once already, and the Bible says he'll do it again, but with fire this time."

"Well, see then, you ain't got nothing to worry about with the water now."

Corporal Robinson felt a hand on his shoulder and turned to see who stood behind him, but there was nothing except empty space and the falling rain hitting him in the face.

"Sam, did you see anybody come up behind me?"

"Nope, I've been shoveling this mud. Robinson, let's get out of here. This mud ain't gonna hold the water back."

Sam no more than finished his sentence before the Rio Grande came crashing over the western dike right behind Robinson. Sloshing through the mud, the soldiers headed for the fort barns and corrals.

"Get out of there!" Corporal Robinson yelled when he passed the corral gates. "The water's coming!" He didn't stop until he reached the stall of his favorite mount and that of his commanding officer, Gen. William T. Sherman. All the while the water rushed through the dike, filling the lower portion of Fort Hancock with its murky depths.

Struggling to lead the horses to higher ground, Corporal Robinson became tangled in the horses' leads. The crash of thunder and water whooshing and swirling around their feet frightened the two younger horses. Robinson fought to control them, but he could not match the frightened, lunging animals in strength. The horses dragged him behind, pulling him under the swiftly running currents.

Fighting for his breath, Corporal Robinson felt the hooves of the frightened horses crushing against his arms and legs. The water pushed him down again and again, until he succumbed to unconsciousness. Unexpectedly, he felt a hand on his shoulder pulling him upward until a great gust of air filled his lungs. Light filled the space around him, and a voice he'd never heard spoke to him.

"It's not time yet. Go about your chores."

Corporal Robinson tried to answer and thank the man for pulling him out of the water, but when he looked around no one stood beside him.

Once on higher ground, Robinson searched for his friend Sam, but he had gone on with some of the other horses. When Robinson reached the upper part of Fort Hancock with his horse and General Sherman's mount, the other troopers slapped him on the back with words of surprise at seeing him alive. General Sherman searched out Robinson to thank him personally.

Sam ran up to his friend and hugged him tightly.

"We couldn't find you anywhere, buddy. What happened to you?"

Robinson related his story to Sam about the man pulling him out of the raging water.

The man shook his head in disbelief. "I swear, Robinson, you got an imagination. I'll say that for you."

About three years after the flood, the blacksmith's stables at Fort Hancock burned. Corporal Robinson became trapped trying to lead the horses out of the burning building. Again, the hand from beyond plucked him from the grip of death to tell his story. Fire and water were Corporal Robinson's fears, but in the end he triumphed over both with special help from an unseen protector.

Fires took out the blacksmith's shop, the carpenter's shop, and the wheelwright's shop. Another incident of fire destroyed the post gymnasium, the quartermaster's stable, and the haystack. Months after the fire, Corporal Robinson's horse threw him and he died, but his ghost roams the area to help victims of fire and flood.

Hancock was frequently flooded by the Rio Grande despite small dams built by the soldiers to prevent this. By the time the last fire at Fort Hancock destroyed most of the wooden structures, the fort had virtually outlived its usefulness. The army turned it over to the Department of the Interior and abandoned it on December 6, 1895.

A town sprang up just east of the fort ruins and the post office opened in 1886, the year the fort's name changed. The town of Fort Hancock today has an estimated population of about two thousand, and it had its fifteen minutes of fame when it was mentioned as a border-crossing point near the end of the movie *The Shawshank Redemption*. Although an eighteen-foot-high fence between the US and Mexican border extends south from El Paso, at Fort Hancock the tall, solid fence ends abruptly and changes into a three-foot-high barbed-wire fence, which unauthorized migrants can easily cross to go over the border.

A historical marker on State Highway 80, fifty-two miles southeast of El Paso, points the way to the site where Fort Hancock once stood.

FORT ELLIOTT

The country was growing. The growth took up the forested area, then the rolling plains with scattered vegetation, and pushed farther west and north, onto the flat, open grasslands with no trees in sight. As the settlers pushed out onto the plains, the army followed and sent soldiers to one last post to rid the frontier of the remaining Indians.

Fort Elliott was built to protect the settlers on the eastern edge of the Texas Panhandle. A Cheyenne attack on white buffalo hunters took place at Adobe Wells, and the installation emerged as a rendezvous point. Maj. James Biddle became commander of 422 troops, including officers and enlisted men, in January 1875.

Dubbed the "Cantonment on the Sweetwater," Fort Elliott was named in honor of Maj. J. A. Elliott. Temporary buildings were put into use in June 1875, and the new fort was ready to begin its service to the army and the settlers in the area. Construction of Fort Elliott's permanent buildings began a month later.

The lumber was hauled in by wagon from Dodge City, Kansas, and the tedious process continued for some time. It took approximately three years to finish the permanent structures. Shortly after the completion of construction, a fire in 1879 destroyed the headquarters, and the work of reconstruction began.

Fort Elliott at one time garrisoned more than four hundred troops, and during the remainder of its usefulness, no fewer than two hundred men were stationed there between 1879 and 1888. The roster of commissioned officers was Anglo-American except one, Lt. Henry Flipper, the first black soldier to graduate from West Point.

Fort Elliott troops' main objective was to patrol the Texas Panhandle as well as the western portion of Indian Territory. They were assigned to stop any of the small bands of Indians from coming into the Panhandle. It made no difference what the Indians were doing in the area; they were to be stopped and turned out of Texas.

During the 1870s many of the Cheyenne, Comanche, and other Indian tribes sought to escape the reservations in the Oklahoma Territory and hide out in the Texas Panhandle.

The security provided by the presence of Fort Elliott brought economic stimulation to the area. By the 1880s huge ranches were developed nearby, and various spreads were grazing as many as three hundred thousand head of cattle.

John Elkinson came from Virginia after the war. In southern Louisiana he encountered his destiny when he met a lovely young girl named Annabel. Their future was assured when she honored him by agreeing to become his wife, but he felt obligated to make a perfect future for the woman of his heart. Elkinson joined an army detachment in Louisiana with the goal of going west to find a fit place to build a home for his beloved Annabel and himself.

The young soldier left his fiancée with her parents until he could search out and secure a place for the two of them. John was a simple man of no means in Virginia, but in Texas, where a man could be as big as his dreams, he was huge.

He longed to have plenty of money and own thousands of head of cattle. John coveted a big house and desired the best of everything for Annabel. In his eyes the tour of duty at Fort Elliott represented a foothold in the land of buffalo, cattle, and limitless opportunities.

John served his country well. He became a decorated hero at Fort Elliott, fighting gallantly and suffering several wounds. John's last injury made him unfit for military duty, and he was discharged shortly afterward with full honors.

Utilizing his skills as a marksman acquired through the army, he hunted buffalo. He sold the hides to the highest bidders to get what he needed for his home and for Annabel.

He needed not only a way to earn money but a stake in the land and opportunities it presented. He found the chance in the industry beginning to dominate the Texas Panhandle: cattle ranching. John took his severance pay from the army and the money he saved from buffalo hunting and invested it in land and cattle. Having amassed several thousand acres of land and several thousand cattle over a long period of time, John felt the time was ripe to send for Annabel. He mailed her a letter with a train ticket enclosed.

While awaiting her arrival, he finished building the most elaborate house in the area and fitted it out with the finest furniture.

His fiancée never reached Fort Elliott. The day before she was to arrive, a mail coach rolled into Fort Elliott. In the bag was a letter for John. Waiting until he was at his home, John took the letter out and read what Annabel had written.

Before anyone knew what had happened, John lost his mind. He wandered off onto the prairie on his favorite horse. When he could not be found, friends went through his home, hoping to discover a clue to his disappearance. Annabel's letter lay on the floor in front of the fireplace, where John had dropped it several days earlier.

Annabel confessed she had never really loved John. She truly thought she'd never do better, but her father introduced her to a man of great financial means several months before. She further confessed she would not be coming to Fort Elliott, for the same day she was to have arrived, she would instead stand at a Louisiana altar and profess her love and loyalty to the rich man she perceived to be a better catch. She told John she hoped he wouldn't hold her actions against her and would think well of her in the future. Above the signature the whole situation was reflected in the words "Your Friend."

John had gone out of his mind with the thought of someone else touching his Annabel. The betrayal of his love was more than he could stand, and John left his house as he had built it. He no longer wanted anything to do with the mansion he'd constructed for Annabel. John rode out the same evening and was never heard from again.

John's ranch, built a few miles from the new railhead, could have made him an even wealthier man than he was. When he disappeared, his hired help left, his cattle scattered to the winds, the mansion fell into disrepair, and his money disappeared as he did.

To this day his ghost is still seen in the area of Fort Elliott, mumbling and riding about the prairie, calling for the beautiful Annabel.

When the railroad passed Fort Elliott by in 1887, it signed the death warrant of the fort. In the summer of 1890, after several years of transferring troops from one post to the next, an outbreak of typhoid fever spread through the soldiers at the fort and hurried along its demise and abandonment.

In October 1890, the gates to Fort Elliott were closed for the last time. The soldiers who marched away on that cool autumn morning remembered many good times and a flourishing area of cattle ranches, now bereft of the buffalo that had roamed there. Many glanced at the small cemetery and thought of those who had fought and died defending the fort and the area. They looked beyond the cemetery, half expecting to see one last time the haunted soul of John Elkinson, who had fought alongside them at one time, or hear his murmured lament blowing across the flat Texas land.

The remaining ruins of Fort Elliott can be visited on South US Highway 152 out of Mobeetie in Wheeler County. One mile west of the intersection of FM 48 the ruins stand deserted. The last surviving items from Fort Elliot are the old wooden flagpole standing at Mobeetie's jail museum, as well as the old jail.

FORT D. A. RUSSELL

The cannon blast at reveille echoes off the mountains around Marfa, Texas. Another day starts as usual. A beautiful horse with his rider in dress uniform trots out onto the parade grounds and they go through their paces. The trooper pulls the horse up and sits atop his mount, watching as the huge military planes roar past overhead. As the last plane of the missing-man formation flies over Fort Russell, Louie and his rider vanish.

The citizens of Presidio County became fearful because of the Mexican Revolution just across the Rio Grande. In order to provide the protection the citizens needed in 1911, the United States established a post first called Camp Albert, renamed Camp Marfa, and later officially renamed Fort Russell. It was named in honor of Gen. David Allen Russell, who fought in the Mexican and Civil Wars. He died fighting for the Union army at Winchester, Virginia.

Fort Russell served the Signal Corps whose biplanes flew over the Rio Grande. Units from Fort Bliss were garrisoned at Fort Russell between 1913 and 1916 for field duties. The fort had to be expanded during World War I to house the extra soldiers. The post became the headquarters for the Marfa Command in 1920, replacing the Big Bend District. Simulated combat maneuvers were conducted at Fort Russell between 1923 and 1936.

After the final name change to Fort Russell on January 1, 1930, Secretary of War Patrick Hurley announced that the fort was to be a permanent establishment. Shortly afterward, in 1931, the government considered abandoning the fort. The Marfa Chamber of Commerce tried to keep the post that gave great economic boosts to the city open during the Great Depression. Marfa lost the fight, and January 2, 1933, saw the last of the troops from Fort Russell gone and the fort in the hands of caretakers.

The final review for the First Dragoons, December 14, 1932, began with an order: "Groom your animals for the last time."

For almost a hundred years, the First Dragoons had set the standards for the US Cavalry, riding to meet any and all enemies, from Mexican revolutionists to Indians. Once their horses were groomed and cleaned each day, the men took their mounts through their paces on the parade grounds. Practicing their drills in front of the review stand had been mandatory the last six months.

"So, they're really shutting us down this time, huh, Sarge?"

"Yep." The drill sergeant didn't look at his men. He knew what he'd see: disappointment, sorrow, and perhaps a little bit of resentment thrown in for good measure. He kept his back to the troops, not wanting his men to see any of the same feelings on his face.

Very shortly they would be saying good-bye to faithful loving friends, the horses that had carried them for many years. Each man had a special relationship with his horse. It would be hard for all of them to say good-bye, especially for him.

He had ridden the same horse for twenty years, and saying farewell to Louie would be the hardest thing he ever did. The men would have a hard enough time without him breaking down in front of them. Nope, he wouldn't let them know how much he was hurting inside. At least their horses were going to be turned out to pasture to live out their lives naturally, but that was not the case for Louie. Louie's fate was sealed much like his own—the only difference was that Sarge would be able to go on living; he just wouldn't be in the army anymore.

Sergeant Hays had known nothing but the army. He had never taken a wife nor had any children. He had served his country, and that's all he knew. This would be his last day in the service, and he had no idea what he was going to do the next day. Louie would not be there to groom, feed, and exercise.

Since he was no longer in the competitive ranks, Louie had only been exercised lightly every day, but it gave Hays something to do in the mornings before he tried to teach the new men horsemanship skills. Tomorrow there wouldn't even be that to look forward to.

Sergeant Hays brushed and groomed Louie's coat until the thirty-year-old horse's hair shined like a new penny in the wintry sunlight. Talking soothingly, Sergeant Hays picked up Louie's feet and brushed the dirt from them and polished them to a high gleam. He painted them with black shoe polish to give them the desired color for the parade grounds. When he was finished with Louie's feet, Hays put a dab of talcum powder in his hand and rubbed it into the star on Louie's forehead and then wiped off the excess with a soft cloth. Louie snuffled at Hays's chest.

"You like that, old friend?"

Using special care, Hays cleaned Louie's nose and around his eyes, and then he rubbed petroleum jelly onto his muzzle to brighten it up.

Sergeant Hays rubbed Louie on the face. "Soon, old boy, it'll be your turn to strut your stuff for the crowd." Louie snuffled at the gentle hands on his face.

Waiting for the regiment to go through their routine, Hays stood beside Louie and watched. Not a horse out of line, they all passed the review stand, both times. The dignitaries saluted the regiment.

Minutes later, Hays turned to his horse.

"It's time to get you ready, Louie." Hays lifted the lightweight saddle up on his faithful companion's back.

Troops in military dress drew their sabers. The gleaming metal glinted in the sun when the soldiers dipped the blades in "hail and farewell."

As the platoons rode past, the colonel and his staff saluted the First Dragons and Troop D. The regiment returned for a second pass faster than before and then faced the review stand for a final salute.

The colonel saluted the troopers and their mounts, made a short speech, and closed the first part of the ceremony for the dragoons. The men stood in front of their horses to say farewell. Each man placed his hand on his horse's face and whispered his own good-bye quietly and personally. Rubbing the noses of the horses, the men remounted and saluted the colonel and the dignitaries again.

When the regiment left the maneuvering grounds, a single horse and rider rode into view. Sergeant Hays in his best dress uniform slowly walked Louie out onto the parade grounds. Louie had been ridden for three championships the year before. The oldest horse in the regiment, he deserved the last review all to himself.

The old man would show all those young whippersnappers how it was supposed to be done. Louie and Hays held their heads high and never made a mistake. Louie's step never faltered. He was as sure-footed as the day he'd begun his training.

Upon completion of their last review, Hays rode Louie through a double row of horses and riders with sabers drawn into the sky. When they passed, the sabers dipped to the ground in fond farewell and respect for the best team in the regiment. Louie bowed his neck proudly and sidestepped slightly at the end of the line, swishing his tail as if to say, "I still have what it takes to be the best."

After the program was over, Hays led the horse to the top of the hill overlooking Fort Russell. There they met with the base veterinarian and Louie chomped his last blade of grass before the vet put him to sleep. Several hours later, he was buried.

On Louie's headstone is the regimental motto, "Animo et Fide," translated meaning, "Friend and Faithful," and it still stands in the Troop B area on top of the small hill. From his resting place, Louie watches as aerial activities from a nearby airbase unfold each day. The one most respected by the people who see it is the missing-man formation. Louie's is not the only story to come out of Fort Russell. Sergeant Hays was a story in his own right.

Shortly after the army decided that Louie should be humanely destroyed, Hays was that same day dismissed from the army. Not knowing what to do with his time, he decided that without the army and Louie, he had nothing to live for, and so he ended his own life. He was found lying next to Louie's grave where he, too, had taken a shot of the same medication the veterinarian had given Louie. Sergeant Hays was not buried on army ground because he had been discharged. However, Sergeant Hays roams the Fort Russell compound looking for Louie. His whistling for the horse can be heard on cold December nights around Marfa.

BUILDING 98,
FORT D. A. RUSSELL

CONSTRUCTED IN 1920, BUILDING 98 HOUSED THE OFFICERS CLUB AND BACHELOR OFFICERS QUARTERS FOR FORT D.A. RUSSELL. DURING THE LATTER YEARS OF WORLD WAR II, FROM 1943 TO 1945, GERMAN PRISONERS OF WAR FROM FIELD MARSHAL ERWIN ROMMEL'S *AFRIKA KORPS* WERE HOUSED AT THE FORT, AND EVIDENCE OF THEIR ORNATE ARTWORK CAN BE FOUND ON THE BUILDING'S INTERIOR WALLS. MURALS DEPICT VIEWS FROM A COURTYARD AND INCLUDE SCENES TYPICAL OF WEST TEXAS. CONSTRUCTED OF ADOBE AND CONCRETE, BUILDING 98 FEATURES A PEBBLEDASH FINISH AND AN A-SHAPED FOOTPRINT, WITH ONE COURTYARD COMPLETELY ENCLOSED AND ANOTHER ENCLOSED ON THREE SIDES

The marker for Building 98 for old Fort D. A. Russell near Marfa

Perhaps the mysterious, glowing orbs of light that sometimes appear in the desert outside of Marfa near Mitchell Flats is Louie, riding on the windswept prairies of West Texas. One can suppose the phantom lights—which are roughly the size of basketballs, and vary in color from white, to blue, to yellow, to red and other colors—are the eyes of the cavalrymen and their horses that lived and trained at Fort Russell. Maybe the lights that hover, merge, twinkle, split in two, flicker, float up into the air, or dart quickly across the sky are the reflection of sabers pointed skyward in honor of Louie and Sergeant Hays as they ride the winds of yesterday into tomorrow.

Fort Russell was re-garrisoned in 1935, and in 1938 officer training began and continued at the fort during the pre–World War II years. In 1943 Fort Russell was established again as a prisoner-of-war camp. Germans who were captured on foreign soil were brought to the United States, and Fort Russell was only one of the internment camps for these men. While I found no evidence of violence with the Germans involved and no ghosts, there are an awful lot of strange languages whispered on those moonlit nights around Marfa. The men and women who worked at Fort Russell wore many different uniforms and insignias, and they had many stories to tell.

In 1944 the first woman officer came to the fort. Civilian women took over as drivers at the fort for the soldiers being shipped overseas. The government closed Fort Russell on October 23, 1946, and ownership was transferred to the Corps of Engineers. In 1949 most of Fort Russell and its facilities were sold to private owners.

In the late 1970s, under the auspices of the Dia Art Foundation, artist Donald Judd purchased the former fort and began converting the buildings. These buildings housed permanent large-scale art installations.

Originally it was to include only the works by Judd, John Chamberlain, and Dan Flavin. The museum was later expanded

to include works by Carl Andre, Ingolfur Arnarrson, Hiroshi Sug-
imoto, Ilya Kabakov, Roni Horn, Claes Oldenburg and Coosje
van Bruggen, David Rabinowitch, and John Wesley. Mr. Judd's
museum opened to the public in 1986 as the Chinati Foundation.

Located at Fort Russell's central complex is Building 98, a
project of the International Woman's Foundation and the home
of the iconic World War II German POW murals. The murals
were completed in 1945 by Hans Jürgen Press and Robert Hum-
pel. Both were German prisoners of war held at Fort Russell. The
building served as the Bachelor Officer Quarters and as an entertainment center for West Point officers during World War I and
the Mexican Revolution. The International Woman's Foundation
took the steps to get Fort Russell on the National Register of Historic Places. The foundation has operated an artist-in-residency
program and base museum since 2002.

In 2002, Mona Blocker Garcia created a foundation for
mature women artists and healthful aging. This movement preserved the important history of Fort Russell to its exact state when
the fort closed. To reach Fort Russell and these museums, take US
Highway 90 out of Marfa toward Fort Stockton for only a couple
of miles. Stay a while and you might be able to witness the Marfa
lights.

BIBLIOGRAPHY

BOOKS

Aston, B. W., and Ira Donathon Taylor. *Along the Texas Forts Trail*, Denton: University of North Texas Press, 1997.

Edmondson, J. R. *The Alamo Story: From History to Current Conflicts*, Plano: Republic of Texas Press, 2000.

Nofi, Albert A. *The Alamo and the Texas War of Independence*, Boston: De Capo Press, 2001.

Pierce, Gerald S. *Texas Under Arms: The Camps, Posts, Forts, and Military Towns of the Republic of Texas*, Austin, TX: Encino, 1969.

Robinson, Charles M. III. *Frontier Forts of Texas*, Lanham, MD: Lone Star Books, June 1986.

Scott, Robert. *After the Alamo*, Plano: Republic of Texas Press, 2000.

Thompson, Frank. *The Alamo: A Cultural History*, Lanham, MD: Taylor Trade Publishing, 2001.

Timanus, Rod. *Illustrated History of Texas Forts*, Lanham, MD: Taylor Trade Publishing, 2001.

Todish, Timothy J., Terry Todish, and Ted Spring. *Alamo Sourcebook, 1836: A Comprehensive Guide to the Battle of the Alamo and the Texas Revolution*, Austin, TX: Eakin Press, 1998.

Tolbert, Frank X. *The Day of San Jacinto*, 2nd ed., Austin, TX: Pemberton Press, 1969.

Wharton, Clarence. *Wharton's History of Fort Bend County*, San Antonio, TX: Naylor, 1939.

WEBSITES

"Ghosts of the Cross Timbers," *Fort Tours*, www.forttours.com.

"Historic Forts and Presidios," *Texas Time Travel*, texastimetravel.com/node/28663.

Kubiak, Len. "Forts in Early-day Texas," *Forts of Texas*, www.forttumbleweed.net/forts.html.

"Old West Forts and Towns in Texas," *Over-land.com*, www.over-land.com/westfort_tx.html.

"Old West Legends: Haunted Forts and Battlegrounds," *Legends of America*, www.legendsofamerica.com.

"Texas Forts," *Texas Escapes*, www.texasescapes.com/Texas-Forts.htm.

The Handbook of Texas Online, https://tshaonline.org/handbook/online.

Wooley, Brian. "The Frontier Forts of Texas," *Texas Almanac*, texasalmanac.com/topics/history/frontier-forts-texas.

Wooster, Robert. "US Army on the Texas Frontier," *Texas Beyond History*, www.texasbeyondhistory.net/forts/military.html.

INDEX

Italicized page numbers indicate photographs.

INDEX

ABOUT THE AUTHOR

Elaine Coleman is an award-winning author whose published books include *Louisiana Haunted Forts, Fat Fannies Fudge Factory, Wolf's Desire, The Gamble, Carl Hall: I Did It My Way, Walt Rambo, Texas Style Bits and Spurs,* and *Tricks, Stunts, and Imposters.* She also has written two family cookbooks and one for her church.

Elaine worked as editor for two independent West Texas newspapers in the 1990s, in which she had her own cooking and fishing columns, and has written for *Reminisce* magazine's "Little House Out Back" column. She owned and operated a cafe at the local cattle auction barn for eight years, where she gathered information for her latest book, *The Trip.*

Mrs. Coleman belongs to the Pecan Valley Genealogy Club in Brownwood, Texas, where she researches for fun and writing. She speaks at various organizations in the surrounding area. Living in and around Taylor and Runnels Counties in Texas all her life, Elaine is proud of the fact that she is a sixth-generation Texan.

Elaine and her husband, Jerry, live on the family farm near Winters, Texas, with three dogs, an old barrel racing horse, and sixty or so mother cows. Besides writing and reading, Elaine enjoys puttering in her garden, quilting, crafting, and working with her husband raising cattle. She also enjoys visits from her children and grandchildren.